By the Grace of God, Blink Once for Yes

By the Grace of God, Blink Once for Yes

CROSSBOOKS
PUBLISHING

Peyton Edwards

CrossBooks™
A Division of LifeWay
1663 Liberty Drive
Bloomington, IN 47403
www.crossbooks.com
Phone: 1-866-879-0502

First published by CrossBooks 04/14/14

ISBN: 978-1-4627-3631-7 (sc)
ISBN: 978-1-4627-3633-1 (hc)
ISBN: 978-1-4627-3632-4 (e)

Library of Congress Control Number: 2014906475

Printed in the United States of America.

This book is printed on acid-free paper.

For my sweet, sweet children.
Without a doubt, I owe you my life.
I love you.

Contents

Preface...viii
Chapter 1   The Beginning...1
Chapter 2   Chasing Love 3
Chapter 3   What I Did Best: Run..6
Chapter 4   A Chance for a New Beginning 9
Chapter 5   Choice 17
Chapter 6   The Journal..26
Chapter 7   The Shadows of Death....................................43
Chapter 8   Blink Once for Yes..47
Chapter 9   General Hospital 53
Chapter 10   Physical and Occupational Therapy 61
Chapter 11   Speech 65
Chapter 12   A Hand of Grace 70
Chapter 13   Going Home 76
Chapter 14   Outpatient Therapy...84
Chapter 15   The Unexpected 89
Chapter 16   A Period of Adjustment..................................93
Chapter 17   A Visit to Rory 103
Chapter 18   The Secret 106

Preface

Five years ago I hated the world and everyone in it. I was depressed, humiliated, timid, and afraid of it—afraid to be noticed. I had three strokes when I was in my prime at the age of twenty-seven that left me much different from how I had been. I was mortified about the disgusting, ugly freak I became overnight. My husband, whom I completely idolized, had an affair and left me behind as a discarded, used-up piece of trash to care for our two young children. I felt even more worthless, if that's possible. I didn't know what to do. I was abandoned by the only person I trusted, and scared of the new me and this new world. It would be a year before I could enter a store and be in the public eye. I felt so humiliated and disfigured, I would have to spend twenty minutes in the car giving myself a pep talk before I'd go in. Tragic, huh?

And then I acknowledged that knocking at my heart. I opened the door and allowed Jesus to come and settle in. I finally relinquished my arrogant, stubborn pride and gave him full access to my heart and mind. Thank God he never got tired of knocking because it was by the grace of God, and God alone, that I watched my life transform before my very eyes. I look back with happiness on that once tragically hateful, bitter, angry girl. I see how God has used my circumstances, my brokenness, to better not only me but those around me to see a modern-day miracle performed before them. I feel such privilege to be able to share God's story with the world.

To have *lived* this story and then get to write it down and actually see how the events connect ... wow. It just leaves me astounded. I am so very grateful that God delights in the broken and uses weakness to magnify his glory. This book is for no other purpose than to magnify God's works, to make them known, and to give him all the glory. I pray that you are not only moved, but that you see God's hand at every turn and realize you are much more than your circumstances. God's abundant grace is there for us to use whenever we need it. All we have to do is humble ourselves and ask. I'm not the same person I was then. Give it all to him, and accept the change. His lens is so much wider than ours. God uses the broken, disadvantaged, weakened people of the world—the "cracked pots," if you will—so that people will know, beyond the shadow of a doubt, that it is him working. We live by the choices that we make, but at every choice we get to choose.

God bless you and your families.

*all the names have been changed, to protect the identities of those involved.

I can do all things through Christ, who strengthens me.
—Philippians 4:13 (NKJV)

Chapter 1

The Beginning

I grew up in a little town on the East Coast, population 534, as an only child. My parents tried for eleven years to have a child. Their prayers were finally answered, and a bouncing baby girl was born on their eleventh anniversary. I came from a very-low-income family. My dad, who passed away when he was fifty-nine, was an underpaid construction worker. But it was a steady paycheck, and he was brought up to live off the land.

We lived in a town that was very big on hunting and fishing. On the first day of bass or hunting season, half the school kids who were old enough didn't even bother to show up for school, male and female alike. Dad hunted and fished every season. In the winter, when he was laid off, we relied on his ability to live off the different game species the land offered. He taught all his nieces and nephews the tricks of the trade and the lay of the land. He had taught me as well. But when I reached sixteen, I became more interested in high school sports and working. I would rather do any of them—and be with boys—than make time for fishing or hunting. I now wish I could have that time back, if only a moment.

My mother was a homemaker. It's funny, because I used to resent that my father would work his tail off from 5:00 a.m. until 8:00 p.m. while *all* she did was clean the house, talk on the phone, and watch soaps. I now see that that wasn't the case. I get it now. The house didn't magically get clean. I respect her. It took twenty-nine years and three strokes to understand, but now I do. My mother and I were never very close. I always despised her for allowing my dad to work so hard. You see, I was more like him—a workaholic. It was a mutual understanding, because I was "Daddy's little girl." But now that I'm forced to stay home right now, I'm getting a better understanding of just what she did. My mom is very good with my children. She gets on the floor and plays hide-and-seek with them. She is far from a rocking-chair grandma. She's my number-one fan and biggest supporter. I honestly don't know what I'd do without her.

Some would say I grew up poor, but never once did that cross my mind. I only knew I was loved, and if you didn't have the cash for it, you simply didn't need it—a policy I still follow today.

I had a traditional childhood, filled with fond memories of playing with friends and my many cousins and going to my grandparents' every other weekend.

I graduated from a small school in 1999. There were only eighty-eight people in our graduating class. It was a place where everyone knew everyone in one way or another, and there was no getting away with anything. Oh, you might think you had kept a secret for the moment, but all you did was buy some time. Just wait until the next day. Not only would your parents know, but the whole town would know!

Chapter 2

Chasing Love

I got into my first serious relationship, like many people, when I was sixteen—mostly because my fellow students said I couldn't date him. I wasn't from the same background as he was. He was only a year ahead of me, and he was the nicest guy. He came from a good, middle-class, Christian family. He was very athletic and absolutely brilliant. When he and his class graduated, I was lost. I was soon to graduate, and he became my high school sweetheart.

His family was very strong in their faith. My own was mostly like the third-generation Israelites'. Something got lost in translation from my highly devoted grandmother to my very ignorant self. I was raised to believe but was never actually taught the whys behind the whats or the ins and outs of the Bible. I had seen a Bible, but Lord knows I had never read one. The tools were there, however. The foundation was just never laid in place. I knew of this Jesus and his father, God. I saw the picture hanging in my grandma's living room, but I didn't know them, not even remotely. I often accompanied my boyfriend and his family to church. I loved it. But even then, I didn't have any real understanding of the Word. I just knew God was real, and that because I was breaking his rules, I'd go to hell. That's just fabulous, really. I completely shied away.

I believed you needed material things to show people you were anything; proving something—I don't know what—to them was important to me. I chased a false sense of reality from early on. I hadn't grown up with anything, but now that I held a job of my own and was going to college and was practically out of the house, I wanted more. I paid for all my wants.

For some reason, I thought I wanted that shiny ring. I thought that ring meant something. I gave it a power it didn't have. My boyfriend knew I wasn't ready; he knew better. He was more informed, thank God. Heck, I knew I wasn't ready, but it didn't matter. I just wanted a ring. Not because it meant something, but because it was pretty and sparkled, and people could see it. I was in love with the idea of being in love. I gave that ring power. But he wasn't about to give in to me, God bless him. I can't exactly remember why it ended, only that it did. And before I knew it, I was planning a wedding to another kid, one I barely knew—chasing the love I was so much in love with—the thought, that is, and that sparkle.

I got married at nineteen, against better judgment, because I was told I couldn't and I shouldn't. All the while, I maintained a full schedule at the local college during the day and waited tables at a small Italian restaurant at night. We were kids in love with the idea of being in love. We had no idea it was so much more than a couple of pretty rings and a piece of paper, or what being married actually meant. He was a year older than I was and came from the same kind of low-income family. Except here's the kicker—his dad was a pastor. His mom and dad had grown to see the proven ways of the Lord and had honored him respectfully since he was, I don't know, seven or eight.

We were married two years after I got out of high school, and before six months were up, we were separated. It set the tone for our young married life. I had my daddy's work ethic and had seen my mom get walked on by people because she was too nice and too timid and meek to defend herself. Well, it made me a bit of a snot. Don't get me wrong. I was a nice girl, but I wasn't afraid to snap that attitude when I felt it was needed. Only now do I see how ugly it was.

We had an on-again/off-again marriage. His parents tried to counsel us and show us the right way, but we just weren't there yet. In no way was either of us ready to accept their teachings or the Word of God. The Bible says to submit to your husband. I'm sorry, but I wasn't having any part of that. I had no idea of the true meaning of the word *submit*, that it didn't mean to bow down and be a doormat. I was determined to rebuke this so-called way of the Lord and had no intentions of submitting to a husband and giving him control over me or my hard-earned money. Oh, heck no. You could say this caused us to butt heads a bit.

We never acted like we were anything more than simply dating, except we had this piece of paper that said we were married and the shiny rings that sparkled to prove it. Neither of us took it seriously. Every six months, we would split up. I would move out, and then six months later, I would come back, only to do the same thing again in a month or two. He was my norm, my comfort blanket. As messed up as our relationship was, it was all either of us knew.

Chapter 3

What I Did Best: Run

Finally, after four years of playing these shenanigans, we said, "Enough." I moved to Alabama to live with my best friend and her husband. I waited tables at a local chain restaurant, and I was very good at it. I smoked pot all day, every day. And a drunken beach trip was generally involved.

I would much rather be stoned drunk than think about my life and take ownership for the sea of my own choices I was drowning in. I was running from responsibility, from ownership, from truth … but to where or what exactly? I was searching for something, but I hadn't a clue what. Or so I thought. I was seeking, but without any proper knowledge. I didn't know what seeking was or what I was seeking for.

I worked four to midnight and then went to the bars until two. Then I went home to do it all over again. For me, it was helping me keep my mask on, the façade that I didn't really care and couldn't be hurt. It was my way to avoid the hurt of reality, that bitter sting only truth can bring.

I flew to Connecticut to meet another friend of mine in March 2005, right after I had moved to Alabama. We flew to California together for spring break on Laguna Beach. I didn't want to go; she had gotten me the ticket for Christmas because I protested. I told her I had no desire to go or to meet a bunch of navy frat boys.

We were going to stay with someone she knew in high school, whom she hadn't seen in eight years. Eight years! Are you kidding me? First our flight was overbooked, so we ended up getting in later and coming in four hours away. Her friend showed up at the airport to pick us up. Being a server, I was very friendly and outgoing, and I extended my hand and said, "Hi, I'm Peyton." A baffled Jackson responded by shaking my hand and saying, "Jackson." I was totally not what he expected, the friend of a friend staying at his house.

Well, because of our flight change our luggage was temporarily missing, so I borrowed a pair of his pajama pants to wear for the night. I could have fit into one leg! At the time I was five feet four inches and one hundred pounds, very physically fit, with short spiky brown hair and sun-kissed olive skin. Jackson is five feet six inches with blond hair, of medium build with a navy beer belly. Needless to say, I was swimming in those pajama pants.

After he gave me the pants, he gave us the queen-size bed in his room to share, and he took the single in the spare room.

We were there for a week. During that week we visited the ocean, Jackson and I went for motorcycle rides and hung out. Jackson and I became very close during the week, despite the fact that I told him I was divorcing and was in no form looking to be a navy guy's story. I was very honest with him and tried to disinterest him and run him off as I did everyone. I tried everything I knew. It didn't work. He didn't care and kept chugging forward. During our talking and getting to know each other, we found out that we were from towns five minutes apart. What are the chances, right? He was from the town right next to my little town where I grew up, in the same area of Connecticut! Shut the front door! We had a lot in common. Despite my efforts to keep him away, we became joined at the hip and made arrangements for him to fly me back down there for two weeks in April to see him.

I came back in April 2005, and we had such a great time

that he invited me back there to live from June to October while he was overseas on duty, to take care of his apartment and two cats. I saw an opportunity to run, to escape yet again, to get away, if only for a minute, to "clear my mind." It required me to transfer restaurants, but that was easy enough. I needed to run, be alone with my thoughts, and be forced to think about my life instead of just masking reality, without the temptation to jump into another relationship. Yeah. That's what I wanted … *right*.

Wrong. Sometimes our circumstances make us want to run, offering the unrealistic temptation of temporary relief. *If I can just get away for a minute, then I'll know what to do, how to proceed.* Wrong again. There is one thing that I cannot outrun, no matter how much I elude the truth or how well I evade the facts at hand: me. I'll always have *me.*

Chapter 4

A Chance for a New Beginning

Enter Jackson. I saw him as my saving grace, my chance to get my act together, and my ticket out. What better chance, right? I'd be moving all the way across the country to California, and he'd soon depart overseas for a few months. How perfect: I'd house-sit for him, live *alone* for a few months, clear my head, be by myself with no distractions or temptations to mask my current situation, and above all, I'd have a chance to run, to be single, to live in a new place, to be Mrs. Nobody! I ran, all right—ran right into a new role.

He was gone literally two days after I arrived, and I knew *no one.*

I started working for the same chain restaurant in California that weekend. It was much slower than I was used to, from the hopping Alabama restaurant. So to make ends meet, I worked literally every single day. I went from making $170 a shift to being lucky if I pulled $40. I didn't mind working every day, because the only people I knew in California were my coworkers at the restaurant. And this way I couldn't get myself into the kind of trouble I had run from—it was perfect.

I became close with a group of girls immediately. In fact, I still see two of them on a regular basis, and I remain in contact with the other two and love them dearly. From that very first night, we were inseparable. We bonded right away; it was as if I had known them all my life. They were the coolest girls I'd ever had the pleasure of knowing. I would hang out with one or all of the girls during the day, and at night after our shifts we would all go to the local bar for an unwinding drink or two.

I talked to Jackson by e-mail every day and every night when I got out of work, and I would e-mail him about my day and vice versa. We got to really know each other. I thought, *this is better. It's a small change but it's a change. I'm getting to know him through e-mail first, because we're worlds apart. This is good, right?* It was nice to not feel rushed, to not jump the gun, but to get to know someone—I mean really get to know him—not just run and jump. It felt right for the first time, like I wasn't hunting love down and forcing it. But I was, wasn't I? Any statistic will show you that emotional relationships of any kind are far worse. They draw your emotions deeper … closer … quicker.

The evening he returned, I got someone to switch shifts with me so I could pick him up. He wasn't even on US soil for twenty-four hours before he got the call that they would be shipping out early the next morning. We had to go buy him all his necessities at the local Walmart because the clothes in his sea bag, which wasn't even unpacked yet, were worn out from months at sea.

He was a crew chief for the Blackhawk squadron and would be riding a hurricane in that was set to make landfall the very next morning. They waited out at sea for hurricane Katrina to touch down and then rode in on helos (helicopters) to start the relief efforts. The hurricane was in the gulf, where it powered up to a category 5 storm. Late in the afternoon of August 28 the helicopters began search-and-rescue operations. He remained on board and in flight until the end of September.

On October 1, I flew to Alabama to pick up my car and the rest of my belongings and drove two hours to the airport to pick Jackson up. Jackson insisted. He didn't approve of the lifestyle I had been leading in Alabama. From there we traveled further up the gulf of southern Alabama to do some house hunting. You see, Jackson had been on sea duty and his rotation was up.

He was being stationed in Alabama and had asked me to join him—as a mere roommate if I wanted. But we had become close over the months of e-mailing, so I did join him and transferred to the same chain restaurant there. This was my chance to begin again, to finally get rid of the masks, tear down the walls I had built up, and wipe the dirty slate clean. I could become something again—someone I liked—and so I did.

We found a gorgeous apartment in a gated community, with a pool and a duck pond. It was like nothing I had ever been privileged to have before. My life was already looking up.

A week later, around October 15, my breasts started really hurting and it occurred to me I was late. I took five pregnancy tests before I believed they were giving me an accurate reading and realized we were pregnant. *Shut the front door!* I went to Jackson one morning before he left for work and presented him with the five tests. Being the stubborn, independent snot I was, I gave him a chance to run and told him I didn't need his permission or support to have this baby; I was very well able to manage on my own. I was very stubborn, and my daddy had taught me to never depend on anyone to get through the game of life, although I had a misconstrued perception of what he actually meant by that; if you wanted something, he said, you had to work for it. And I did. I have a very strong work ethic. Jackson said he didn't want to run; he wanted to be in our lives. Given my not-so-steady past, I made the hard choice to believe him.

He proposed marriage three times before I accepted. I didn't want to be remarried, let alone for a child. But Jackson insisted to me that that was not why he wanted to get married. Ah, but first I had to take care of my pending divorce in Connecticut. I had only run from and successfully evaded it; I had never actually made it final—officially.

So I did, and it went rather smoothly and quickly. True

to my nature, we were married in Alabama at the courthouse before the ink was even dry on my Connecticut divorce. Then we were married again in Connecticut in front of our select family because, you see, my dad was dying of lung cancer, and I wanted him there.

We had a baby shower two days later. Why is this relevant, you ask? Because that was the last time I saw my father alive. I was eight months pregnant. He was fifty-nine; he passed away from Cancer two weeks later. My dad was so looking forward to meeting his first grandchild. He held on as long as he could. He died thirty years to the date after his mother.

A month later, in July, my son Noah Michael was born. He saved me; I was the epitome of a daddy's little girl. I loved my father very much and was very close with him, and quite frankly, under normal circumstances his death would have destroyed me. If it hadn't been for my sweet, sweet boy, they would have found me overdosed in an alley somewhere, masking my pain.

There's no doubt in my mind that God saved me that day by blessing me with my beautiful son. He gave me something to divert my attention, something to really grasp and divert all of my focus. He gave me a purpose, a new job. I became someone, a mom. I may have given birth to him, but he birthed me. *This* is who I was born to be. Everything changed from there. I had no desire to run, to ever be anything but a mother and a wife. I starred in the role immediately of a young devoted wife, mother, and server—never a dull moment.

The same weekend I gave birth to Noah, we closed on our first house. It was in a good neighborhood just outside the city. It was all one level, and had three bedrooms and two baths with a fenced-in yard and a garage. It wasn't a brand new house by any means, but we gutted and painted it made it to our liking. It was perfect. It was a perfect place for us to start our family, to begin our life, to forget the past and the masking facades it held. This was my chance to take pride in my role as mother and wife and have a "real" marriage, meaning more than just a couple of rings.

In fact, this time I didn't even want the shiny, expensive sparkle. I was surprised, but I just wanted a plain band. I know, right? Weird! Pregnant and filled with bliss (a.k.a. hormones) I was more interested in Noah and the family, and in being a good mother, wife, and family person. And I was.

Within the next nineteen months I cared for Noah during the day, which normally ran 6:00 a.m. to 4:00 p.m.; he was on his father's military schedule. Then at night I would work as a server/bartender at the local chain restaurant. Often my work night would end between 11:00 p.m. and 2:30 a.m. I liked being a mom and a navy wife, and I liked my job. I was good at it—no, I was great at it, and I prided myself on my family. The ultimate supermom, I took care of my family and my house, and still held down a job. I was nothing if not devoted to my family and my work. I took my titles seriously. Above all, my family came first; I was a wife and a mother, and everyone knew it. I wouldn't learn till many years later that there are no supers and no titles; they're overrated. I felt good about myself when I worked, when I produced. I got my significance out of what I did. God doesn't want us to get our worth and value out of what we do. We are all human. I'm human.

Jackson and Noah, generally flanked by his friend David, would come to the restaurant for dinner at least five out of the six days a week I worked. Everyone knew I was happily married with a beautiful, bouncing baby boy.

We did everything as a family—everything: paying bills, shopping, grocery shopping, cleaning. We were a military family through and through, as close as they come, but we also had our standard issues that come from being in a military family. We were away from any family and used to the coming and going of friends. We made friendships that would last, but more important, we were forced to rely on one another, be one another's best friend, one another's everything, and we were.

In July, I became pregnant again, and I delivered a beautiful little girl, Emma Grace, forty weeks to the date. After I delivered, I began working at another restaurant during the day. So it was babies, house, and restaurant number two during the day and then restaurant number one most nights. My sweet girl was born in May, and Jackson's time in Alabama was up in November. We were being relocated, heading back to California to serve another sea duty tour. Jackson was due to ship overseas in January. I was sad to leave my life, but happy to go back to my California family.

I was sad about Jackson leaving in January, but we had agreed I would take a leave of absence from work while he was gone. There was no way I could work and manage a house and two kids younger than two. I would be working to pay the sitter, which would have just been silly. It was a very stressful time: a new baby, a semi-new town, some new people, moving, finding a house, and so on.

We left for California the second week of November. I had been having a constant headache that would not go away for a couple of weeks. On the drive through Alabama, it started to get extremely worse. I started to become sleepy, to the point that I could barely hold my eyes open any longer. I was having the onset of a bad migraine, or so I thought. I called Jackson, who was in the truck right in front of me, and told him I needed to stop. He told me the airport was only ten minutes away. We were headed there to pick up his dad, who was flying in to help us drive to California and renovate the house. I didn't think I would make it ten more minutes. It was only a two-hour drive. It was crazy; you would have thought I'd been driving all day, not just two hours. We didn't even make it out of Alabama.

We finally got to the hotel and Jackson got me all set up. He closed the window curtains, making the room dark, took the kids, and went to get his father from the airport while I took migraine medicine and attempted to sleep the headache away. The hotel rooms were adjoining, so Jackson took our six-month-old and our two-year-old over to his father's room, had dinner over there, and visited with the little ones until they fell asleep.

The next morning, I woke and felt refreshed: migraine gone. However, I still had a persistent mild headache that just would not go away. Excedrin Migraine became my friend, but it brought only temporary relief.

We had rented our house in Alabama to some friends who were also in the navy, and had rented a house in California from a navy chief. Jackson had a knack for finding houses I hated, needing a little "TLC." This one was no different. The previous tenant had not taken care of the house, so we spent our first two weeks there gutting and painting the house just to make it livable for our family. This house was disgusting when we walked through it. Alcohol had been spilled everywhere, there were animal urine stains all over the carpet, the paint and fixtures were awful, and I walked out with five flea bites.

When we were finished, it was a beautiful house. Well, we weren't really finished, but it had new carpet and paint and fixtures. We had made our mark: the house was beautifully transformed.

The night of December 5, I stayed up till two in the morning finishing painting our son's room. It was the last one to need finishing.

We spent the day of December 6 lounging about the house with our family. We put Emma in a cute dress and proceeded to try to get a good photo of her. Jackson would position her this way and that way, and throw her up in the air, trying to get a giggle while I manned the camera.

After we were finished with pictures, we had lunch and settled down on the couch. I was holding Emma and as usual had put her to sleep. Jackson began teasing me about always getting to hold her and snuggle her while she slept, so I gave her to him and got up to go to the bathroom. I was hit with severe vertigo and fell to the floor.

Jackson said, "What's wrong? You okay?"

I said, "The room's spinning. I'm really dizzy. I think I'm having a really bad migraine." They had never done that to me before.

I proceeded to combat-crawl on all fours to my bedroom, right around the corner, and try to sleep it off. That's how it usually went: the migraine would totally incapacitate me, I'd take the prescribed meds, and I'd sleep it off in a dark room. But this was way different.

I started getting migraines when Noah was six months old. I had had one about every six months, so I hadn't really become too experienced with them, but I had had enough.

Chapter 5

Choice

I want you to lie down in your bed, flat on your back, arms down by your sides. Don't move a muscle—not your tongue, your lips. Don't swallow, twitch your nose, or move your fingers—nothing but your eyes. Only vertical eye movement—that is, up and down ... ah, ah, ah, don't look to the side, just up and down—no peripheral, open and shut. Listen. Listen to the gentle hum of the fan; the buzz of the air conditioner; the thunderous tick tock, tick tock of that second hand on the clock on the wall; the sound of the flesh of a fidgeting person sticking to a chair; the drip, drip, drip of the different medications hanging and going into your IVs. Notice the brightness of the lights and the darkness of the shades being drawn, the way the shadows fall and form on the wall.

Hear people talking all around you, over you, like you're part of the furniture ... a mere decoration. Nurses and doctors talk in the hallway, and when they come into the room, they acknowledge that you're a vegetable in the bed but proceed to talk over you and at you instead of to you. You're locked in, trapped in your own body, unable to move a muscle. You can communicate only by a system of blinking your eyes. One other person—*one*—believes you are actually communicating. The doctors believe you to be brain-dead and are just amusing that one other person but don't truly believe you're still in there. Suddenly the IQ and respect you worked so hard to gain mean nothing. Because you can't speak or move, you obviously aren't there, they don't believe. It is wishful thinking for that other person to think you are actually communicating with them. They are just random, per-chance blinks. They mean nothing. You're brain-dead. It is time to let go.

But wait: a flicker on the monitor … Could it be? Are you there? Oh, wow. Oops—we almost killed you because we didn't believe you were there. Yeah, oops.

I was very happy with my life, and yet through no fault of my own I was forced to start, literally, all over again. You know those things you take for granted every day like waking up, stretching, showering, going to the bathroom, brushing your teeth, cleaning your ears—everyday personal hygiene? I had to relearn *everything all over*! From the simple licking of my lips, to being potty trained again at twenty-seven, to walking, to just being me—*everything.*

Every day is filled with emotional turmoil I cannot control. However, I can *choose* to control how I look at it and respond to it. I am a firm believer that we live by the choices we make. We may not be in control of the circumstances, but we are in control of how we allow them to play out. Don't be anybody's victim, not even your own.

My name is Peyton Edwards. I am thirty-two. At twenty-seven I had three strokes: one blood clot, a brain-stem dissection in the basilar artery, one of the two arteries housed in the brain stem, and a dissection of a blood vessel in the left lobe of my brain. I should be dead or a vegetable at the least. That dissection in the left lobe of my brain saved my life. It caused the blood in my brain to "back flow." They have no idea why I had a stroke, let alone three. More important, they have no idea how I survived. I do: it was by the grace of God.

I had just moved with my husband at the time to California.

We'd been there two weeks. It was a usual beautiful day at the beginning of December.

Where'd we leave off? Oh yes. So I combat-crawled, on all fours, to my bedroom to sleep off what we thought at the time was a migraine. I awoke in the middle of the night and realized that my left side was numb and I was very nauseated. I got up to go to the bathroom and fell right off the toilet because the left side of my body was tingly and weak. I screamed to Jackson for help, he came find me on the bathroom floor, got me up and dialed 911. The ambulance arrived, and the paramedic crew assessed me and took me to the closest emergency room, four miles from our house. The doctor at the hospital did a quick CT scan, stopping just above the brain stem, and said I was a twenty-seven-year-old with a migraine. They gave me a shot of morphine for the pain and some pills for the nausea. Then they sent me out the door, releasing me into my husband's care.

As soon as the pain medicine wore off the next day, I became nauseated again. This time my whole body was tingly and achy. Strange, right? I spent the morning lying on the cold tile floor of the upstairs bathroom. The coldness comforted me, and it was too hard to crawl back to the toilet when I needed it.

This time my husband took me into the same ER, where they sat me in a closet like booth, rocking back and forth, shivering and screaming, "Make the dizziness stop." Seriously, it was like a little ten-by-ten-foot room with only a chair and, thank God, a garbage can to vomit in! No pillow, no blanket. The doctor came in and said, "Oh, you have a history of migraines. Follow up with a neurologist." No scans or workups, just a brief history. They gave me a shot of morphine and sent me packing. They had to wheel me out to the car because I was still weak from the morphine, which was enough to knock out my 230-pound husband. I weighed in at ninety-seven pounds!

Walgreens was right next door, so we went to drop off my

prescriptions, and then Jackson took me home, complaining of a headache, and got me settled upstairs in my two-year-old son's bed, because it had toddler rails. Then he went to pick up my prescriptions and get the kids from a neighboring navy family. Now would be the time to mention that they discharged me with the wrong name on the paperwork. Jackson called the ER, concerned, to inform them of this and make sure everything was okay. They blew it off and said it was no big deal; it was merely the name of the gentleman released before me, Jackson was told; it happened all the time. Everything else was right, so it was fine.

He came back, gave me the prescription pain medicine and migraine medicine, put the baby monitor next to me, and let me sleep it off.

I had every sign, every symptom of the onset of locked-in syndrome listed in any study, but they were unwilling to think outside the box. Strokes don't happen to young people, right? You need to be elderly, not a young twenty-seven-year-old mother of two, but like a grandma or grandpa in their seventies or eighties.

Jackson came in early the next morning after he had gotten the babies settled, and gave me a piece of cold pizza. As I was chewing and attempting to carry on a conversation with him, he noticed that my speech was slurred and the right side of my face had drooped. At first he thought, *whew—thank God,* because my slurred speech could be explained by the medicine. An immediate swell of relief flowed through him. Then he squeezed my left hand, and I felt it. But what about the drooping face? There was no explanation for it. And soon I made him aware that I couldn't feel or move my entire right side. I asked him, "What does this mean? What's happening to me? Why don't I sound normal?" Trained not to panic and to maintain composure in less than normal situations, he never let on that my face was drooping or that he was worried. He just said we should call 911 yet again, because the pain was increasing and not decreasing.

The same guys from the first day arrived, saying, "What are you doing home?" I remember them picking me up and carrying me downstairs, because we had just moved in and the boxes in the hallway prevented them from bringing a stretcher upstairs. They carried me down two flights of stairs to the awaiting stretcher. Noah, then two years old, was very concerned. He watched as the EMTs loaded me into the ambulance and screamed for Mommy. Our navy friends conveniently lived two minutes around the block and swung over to grab him and the baby. That was the last time I saw our beautiful California home.

The ambulance took me the four miles down the road to the same ER, where one of the paramedics told the male nurse, "I have a stroke victim here." That nurse, who had checked me in the day before, said, "No, she's been here twice already. She's a mental case, a morphine addict" and proceeded to set me in the hallway for *three hours*! Didn't even assess me! Said I was *faking everything*. Once you're labeled a drug seeker, everyone on staff ignores you; you're a "troll," and they have better things to do.

I knew they weren't taking me seriously when a boy came in with a fractured arm and was seen and released while I was still on a stretcher on the right side of the narrow hall. I was tired, so tired, I begged and pleaded with Jackson to just take me home. Thankfully, he wouldn't hear of it and made me wait. It wasn't like I could go anywhere on my own.

A sweet little old lady and her sister overheard me talking to my husband. They stopped to ask what was going on and if they could pray with me. Her husband was a minister for one of the local churches and was in a room down the hall. She was in disbelief that I was sitting on a stretcher, in the hallway, on my third visit. She brought me a blanket from her husband's room because I was cold and the staff was boycotting me for some reason unknown to me at the time.

At one point Jackson went to the front desk and demanded that I at least be assessed; he got a little loud with them.

It wasn't until shift change that a first-year resident heard me talking to the sweet little old pastor's wife and her sister and noticed the slurring in my speech and the droopiness in my face and stopped by the foot of my gurney. I swore to her this wasn't my normal speech and said I didn't know what was going on.

Finally! She ran a pen up my feet. They didn't even twitch, but let me tell you, I felt it. She continued to assess me, and sent me immediately for a CT scan. I can remember them running me down the hill outside to get to the building the CT machine was in and taking off my jewelry. What do you know—I had had two strokes. They admitted me.

I was fading in and out of consciousness. The next thing I knew, I woke in a room where a small pregnant woman said in a very melancholy tone, "You've had two strokes: one roughly two weeks ago, remember when I thought I was having a severe migraine on the way to California – it was actually a blood clot; and it looks like another one two days ago." Oh, wait: you mean, as in two days ago when I first came to the ER by ambulance and Dr. Rodriguez sent me home! Perfect. Just great.

By that time I was going into shock, and I remember finding it weird that I didn't really care. I was just tired, completely at peace. Jackson came into the room where I had been taken after the CT scans and was completely beside himself, bawling his bloody eyes out. I had no cares in the world. I was like, "Ah, I had two strokes. It's okay." He looked at me, sobbing, and said, "Oh God, they have to know: if anything should happen, do you want any heroic efforts attempted?"

I remember not feeling anything, nothing at all, finding it strange because I knew I should—obviously—but even then, I didn't. The strongest military man I knew was sobbing at my bedside, and I had not a single care in the world. I told him, "No, no heroics," and he sobbed, "Oh God."

That was the very last thing I remember until waking for brief periods of time a day later.

The following day I briefly remember Jackson coming to talk to me about what the doctors were discussing with him. He was very good at keeping me well informed of every move and made sure to include me in every decision. I didn't necessarily grasp everything he was telling me, but I trusted him and had complete faith in him.

He was my advocate; he spent every waking moment doing research so he knew what he was talking about and was prepared to counter the doctors' every decision.

They convinced Jackson that I was in good hands, with plenty of staff around me should something come up. He should go home to the babies and get some much-needed rest, they said; he hadn't slept at all. So he did, saying, "If anything comes up, I'm only five minutes away. Call me. Let her know I didn't leave."

That night the night nurse assessed me and I was unresponsive. He thought I was sleeping, but to my knowledge I was talking to him the entire time and doing as he asked. He told me to blink my eyes—I blinked. To squeeze his hand—I squeezed. To wiggle my toes—I wiggled. I was in the middle of talking to him when the punk turned and walked away.

Little did I know I had had yet another stroke, and that the reason he couldn't hear me or see me move anything was that I wasn't doing any of those things.

The next morning, Jackson came in to find I had taken a turn for the worse. I had had yet another stroke, and this one was another dissection but in the left part of my brain, making me a completely locked-in quadriplegic.

The doctors told him after my third stroke that there wasn't any hope. If I survived, I'd be a brain-dead vegetable, a locked-in quadriplegic for the rest of my life, and would have no quality of life. *If* I survived. *If* ... At twenty-seven, the prime of my life, I would never be anything more than frozen, a vegetable.

Jackson wouldn't accept that. He searched and found another opinion. Dr. Morgan Shepard told him there was a very dangerous procedure he could try. It would either flat-out kill me or it would help me survive and to live a life with quality.

Jackson knew I didn't want to be a locked-in quad, knew he had to make a choice. What choice, really? Death would be far more of what I wanted than remaining a vegetable. He had to act fast.

He made the decision to trust Dr. Shepard. Either death or a vegetative state awaited me, but first I had to show them, the doctors, that I was there.

The doctors and the nurses came in and tried to get me to make some movement, some response, anything to let them know I was there. I wouldn't respond to them. Jackson came over, grabbed my hand, and started talking to me. Within moments, my eyes shot open and I began responding to *him* and him alone. The deeply rooted connection we shared was unbelievable. From the very beginning, only he could get a response from me, and only he knew, beyond a reasonable doubt, that I was there.

He had this control, this way about him that I responded to even as I was in the coma. I would get all worked up, with my blood pressure elevated, and that would send the machines buzzing. The nurses would try to soothe me and couldn't. They would call Jackson in, and he'd grab my hand and whisper in my ear. Slowly everything would calm down and the buzzing would stop. We were one.

And so began the hardest test of my adult life. Jackson kept a journal for the next two weeks when I was in a coma, to keep track of events. He also brought in my iPod and placed the ear buds in my ears so that I wouldn't feel lonely. I would always have my favorite country music band to listen to.

God love him, the day I woke up, I couldn't wait for someone to take those wretched things out! The nurse took them off to wash my hair, as to not get them wet; she wanted to get me "nice and pretty" for family to see me, she said. And I thought, *Oh, thank God.*

My neck was hurting, and she must have seen the pain crinkling my forehead, because she let me know that I had a fresh incision that would be a little sore for a while. Dr. Akshadha had had to insert a tracheotomy tube so that I could breathe. She talked to me throughout my entire bath and hair washing. I could feel her wash my hair. I felt like I was going to drown. I could feel her wash my body, yet it was numb. It didn't feel like mine.

So, the incision explained the sharp pain in my neck, but why couldn't I breathe? Why did I need this tube in my throat?

I thought I'd finally gotten rid of the nonstop music playing over and over, but wouldn't you know that sweet little nurse *put the ear buds back in* when she was finished. She was just doing her job, and although I was screaming at her not to do it, I had no way of making her hear my cries. I got out a few moans when she turned me to wash my hair, but that was because I had a fresh incision and this big, bulky, uncomfortable tube sticking outta my neck!

Needless to say, the day I woke, they removed the ear buds. I was so very grateful and I didn't listen to music, of any kind, for a year and a half!

Chapter 6

The Journal

This is the journal Jackson kept while I was in the coma:

6 December

Around 6:00 p.m. we were sitting on the couch. I had been giving you a hard time for always being the one to put Emma to sleep. You caved in and gave her up. As you stood up, you fell over. You said it was a spinning feeling along with your left side feeling tingly. I had told you to lie down in the bedroom and get some sleep. Later that night, I checked on you to see how you were doing, but you had been sleeping fairly calmly.

7 December

Early in the morning, around 4:00 a.m. or so, you woke up to go to the bathroom. You started screaming, "Make the spinning stop! Make it stop! It hurts!" You couldn't stay on the toilet because your left side was still tingly. I came over, laid you on the bathroom floor, and looked you over for bites, bruises, or any sign of prior injury. You could squeeze with both hands and were talking with pain/excitement but normally. I didn't like how there was no explanation for what was happening, and it had lasted long past your typical migraine. So I called 911 (both kids were still asleep). EMTs showed up about five or ten minutes later. They got you up on the bed and assessed you, but found nothing different. They took you to the ER, five minutes down the road.

At this point I called Diane, but no one answered. It was 6:30 a.m. I called Paul, and he came over in about fifteen to twenty minutes. I had the kids all set for when he got there, and I took off. When I got there, you were already back in the ER. I had to fill out insurance paperwork, and then I came back. At this point you had already had a CT scan of your head, and blood work, and were getting Demerol for the pain and Benadryl for any infection and something for nausea. Dr. Rodriguez, the on-call ER doctor, came back to ask a few questions and said that the CT scan was normal. He wasn't sure what had caused the left side to be numb and tingly but prescribed Maxalt after another Demerol dose before we were discharged. He said to follow up with our doctor for severe headaches. Our nurse was friendly and very helpful. As we were dropping off the prescription at Walgreens, we realized the discharge paperwork we had wasn't even ours. We called to inquire, but they said it was no big deal. I got you home, laid you in bed, kept it quiet, and picked up your prescription with Paul and the kids. Came back to give you the Maxalt, which was not to be taken with anything else, so I gave you one pill.

Two hours later you said the pain was worse. I called the ER and asked. They said to take it as directed and follow up with the doctor later. So four hours after the first dose I gave you a follow-up dose. You were finally able to sleep (I think because of pain more than anything). Also the appointment with the base doctor was scheduled for Thursday.

8 December

Today the tingling was gone, but your whole body was in pain. We tried to deal with it the best we could, but nothing helped. I called the ER again to ask what we could do. They told us to follow up with our doctor. I explained that the situation had gotten worse and they asked the on-call doctor—so they said—if you could be admitted for further evaluation. We waited until about 9:00 a.m. and you couldn't take it anymore. By that time you were living in the bathroom, lying on the cool tile of the floor, shaking with the chills but dry heaving so frequently that it became pointless to keep dragging yourself back and forth between the bedroom and bathroom. I got the kids packed up and everybody loaded in the truck and headed back to the ER.

When we got there, I parked in front of the ER and left the truck running with the kids in it. I carried you in. They told me to fill out paperwork and that it would be a while. I had just called and been told they would bring you right in. So I told them you were in severe pain and had gone into convulsions on the toilet. They took you right back, at which point I took the kids to Diane's. I was back in about an hour and a half. I asked to go and see you, and the lady at the desk said she did not see you, that you must be back getting some tests done. So I filled out the insurance paperwork again.

A half hour or so later, I finally got back there, only to find you in a closet like room and not having even been assessed yet! *No* blanket, *no* vomit bucket, *no* nurse, *nothing* at all and *nothing* done and it had been this long. I went and found you a blanket. You were shivering and had ahold of a trash can because you were dry heaving.

I stayed in with you, waiting for someone to come in. After what seemed like an eternity, I went looking. I had noticed the board on the wall the day before for tracking patients, nurses, and doctors along with priority. I looked at it today to find that your name was by itself—no nurse assigned, no doctor, nothing. At that point I calmly went to the nursing counter to ask for you. None of them knew you or said they knew why you were there or where you were. By now I was *furious*! I demanded that someone assess you and give you the care we were promised and deserved. They all replied, "Just as soon as we can. She just has a migraine." An hour later they came back, after constant bugging from me. They put you in the bed and gave you 2 mg of morphine, which knocked you out and cured (masked) all your symptoms, including the ability to tell the doctor what was wrong. After the morphine wore off, they asked for a urine sample. The nurse and I wheeled you over to the bathroom, and I carried you in. At this time we found that you had started your cycle. When we got back to the bed, the nurse was disgusted that there was blood in the container, and we explained why.

As soon as you lay down (because sitting made you nauseated from the spinning), you yelled that you were still in extreme pain. They gave you a second shot of 2 mg of morphine. Undoubtedly you fell pretty much right to sleep. While you were sleeping, Dr. Garrison, the on-call ER doctor, came in and said you have a UTI, and that this was what was causing your migraine. I had asked about another CT scan, MRI, or spinal tap—something to figure out why this was lasting so long. He told me the blood work was good and that you had a CT scan done yesterday—no sense in spending extra money. I assured him that insurance was covering it and that he should do whatever it took. He said no, she has a UTI follow-up with a neurologist.

Well, you were still sleeping, and we have an appointment with base on Thursday to get a referral, but it was not good enough for me. I called TRICARE on base and talked to a nurse named Bill. He gave me a list of neurologists in the area and said he would try to walk a referral through. I called everyone and had an appointment set up with Liam Parker on Thursday. Half an hour later, they called back and said they could get us in tomorrow, Tuesday, at 3:00 p.m. I talked to Bill again, and he said the referral went through with no problems. When I went back in to see you, you were just waking up. The nurse had come back to tell us to follow up with a neurologist but that no one would be available until February. I had told her we already had an appointment with Liam Parker tomorrow. She walked away. About half an hour later, Dr. Garrison came back to ask how I knew Liam Parker, because there was no way I had an appointment otherwise. I told him I didn't know him; I just *called*. He shrugged and gave us a prescription for cypro—an antibiotic for the UTI and Loratab for the pain. He said he was going to give you 2mg more of morphine (now the third!) right before you left. Five minutes later, we wheeled you out the door (passed out due to the shot of morphine!). Around 6:00 p.m. or so, the morphine finally wore off, at which point you were in severe pain. I called back to the ER, and the nurse I talked she suggested giving you the Loratab prescribed and following up with the neurologist tomorrow. At this point I guess I accepted that response because it made more sense than a UTI and you have a history with migraines, though never *this* bad, but maybe it is possible. So I gave you Loratabs, some apple juice, and cold pizza—it is what you wanted—after which, you fell asleep.

Today was also the day my dad was flying down to help with the kids while you were in the hospital and while you were sick.

9 December

About 9:00 a.m., after the kids were up and on routine—I had checked on you before through the night and had the babies' monitor on—I went up to their room to check on you. You were crying, drowsy, and in pain. I immediately noticed that the *right* side of your face was drooped and you had slurred speech. I assessed you. Your breathing was a littler more shallow, your eyes reacted fine, but you could not control the right side of your body. I immediately called 911; the EMTs showed up ten minutes later. I gave them your full history, explained what state you were in then and now, and they took you right in. I packed up the kids to Diane's again (actually Tom packed them up and I brought their stuff over). I was at the ER in about an hour and a half.

Around 11:00/11:30 a.m., I asked to go back to see you, but they said no. I asked every five minutes, but they still said no. Twenty minutes later, they had me fill out paperwork and still would not let me go back. I pleaded with them to please let me be with you. Finally one RN let me back. As soon as I got back, I found you were *on a bed in the hallway! You had not been assessed! Are you kidding?* I went right to the nurses (all the same nurses from previous days—they know us well by now), and they said they would be right with me. Doctors and nurses were the same—walking by us like we were homeless asking for money! They would look and then stare away as they walked by.

I caught one nurse and asked her to please help me and my wife. I said she had been in pain for three days, gotten worse, has slurred speech, help us. She said the ER is meant for those who are in dying pain and immediate emergency. I said, "Look at her!" She walked *away*! I grabbed the next nurse and asked, "Why haven't we been seen yet?" She said the doctor knew she came in Sunday with her left side tingling and a migraine, and then again on Monday with no tingle but with full-body aches and a migraine. Now it was her right side … It was probably a psych case where she's convincing herself to make pain. I was *furious*! She walked away before I could finish a sentence.

A little bit later, you had to go to the bathroom. I had asked that same nurse for a wheelchair, and she said there was none available. I then asked her for assistance to help carry you to the bathroom. She said no, she didn't have the time, and *walked away*! So I picked you up and carried you to the bathroom, and *none* of the nurses and doctors so much as raised an eyebrow or asked if you or I needed anything. When we got back to the hallway, I went to another nurse, demanding treatment for you. The security guard approached. I pretty much said, "You will not lay a hand on me!" I turned and found a nurse and asked for help. When I got back to you, no one had come yet. I called Bill, the on-base RN from yesterday, and he said to ask for an assessment. They are required to do that as many times as necessary. After I asked a different nurse, they checked your blood pressure and temperature and then she walked away!

Right afterward, several rooms had filled and cleared several times, but a couple of visitors of another patient had been hearing everything. She came over, said her husband was a minister, and that what was happening to us was sad. She asked to say a prayer with us right there in the hallway. I was still asking for help and pleading with everyone. At shift change around 3:30 p.m., a first-year resident doctor came up and asked us what was wrong. I told her everything. She did a full assessment on you, which hadn't yet been done today or any previous days. Fifteen minutes later, she insisted you be taken to MRI/A+ STAT!

Right about this time, my dad was just getting in, so I went to the house with him, got him set up with the kids from Diane's, and came back to the hospital. When I came back, the night-shift RN grabbed my arm with sympathy and told me where you were (finally in a room, but now I'm scared). I walked in and you said—still slurred—"It's not good, babe. It's not good. I had a stroke …" The resident came in and explained that there had been a chronic stroke two to three weeks prior (on the way down) and another one two to three *days* before today. This meant Saturday or Sunday, which is what we first brought you in for! I didn't know what to do or say. They said if you had family, now would be the time to have them come … so I called your mom and everybody … My mom and your mom were getting ready to leave Wednesday. Around 8:30 p.m., they took you up to ICU bed 8. The first night I stayed with you …

10 December

Busy day. First full day in ICU. The nurses are nice. There's a lot of talking between you and I. We came up with hand signals in case it became too hard for you to talk. I brought the kids in to see you. Noah didn't understand—I told him you had a boo-boo. A lot of tests; a second MRI to try to get more information. Unfortunately, it gave the same vague results. We didn't know if it was a dissection or a thrombus stroke. That night there was a new nurse. He said he had gotten in trouble for letting visitors stay overnight, so he made me leave. The last thing you had said to me was that you were not ready to die and for me to please not go. (I am trying with all my strength to hold it together—it is so incredibly hard!) I called and checked on you every two hours.

11 December

Today I came in to find out some bad news ... Things had taken a turn for the worse last night. You had gone from right-side paralysis and slurred speech to full-body paralysis, no speech—only communication through your eyes. You were locked in your own body ... They put you on the list for another MRI to see what had happened. As you went down, Dr. Akshadha (your doctor since we had been in ICU) said this does not look good and that I need to prepare myself for the worse. I called my dad and asked him to take the kids to Diane's so he could come in; I needed someone. Also the doctor who did your first MRI had come up to check on you. We all went down to where they were going to do the MRI. Caseworkers from TRICARE from base had shown up (very nice and helpful) to see if we needed anything. When Dad showed up, so did Paul and Tom.

About a half hour into your MRI, one of the techs came out to say you had one more test. Just then I heard Paul yell,

"George! Are you okay?" [George is Jackson father.] I looked over to find him grabbing his chest, falling over … Okay, we definitely didn't need this. I told the tech we needed some help; I wasn't sure if it was a heart attack. Your nurse came right over. We calmed him down, but I want him checked out anyway. So I was in there with you, and they were wheeling Dad into the same ER that gave us such problems.

Kind of a rough day so far, but I was doing my best to stay strong and suck this up, because I could not break down now! You had finished your test and we were heading up. On the way, I checked in on Dad to ensure he was okay. The results came back four hours later. We were communicating through eye movements—a system of blinks. When Dr. Akshadha came in, he asked me to step into the other room with him. He said you had had another stroke, and that it did not look good. He was not sure anything could be done. It was just a matter of time, and if you did survive, you would be a locked-in quadriplegic. I broke down … He then asked what efforts should be given to bring you back if your heart stopped. I cried even harder … took a deep breath, tried to get it together. Came back to you and had the hardest conversation of my life—through eye communication. I told you what they found and explained that if we pulled through, they thought you would be paralyzed forever. I asked if you wanted to be brought back like that, and you said no … I told you no matter what, you were to keep fighting and that until it was over for good, I would not stop either (crying on you the whole time). I said if it came to that, I would take care of your mother, the kids would know you, and you would lie next to your father.

After about fifteen to twenty minutes, I went to Dr. Akshadha and told him no heroic efforts would be done to bring you back. I had also told Dad to get the kids here as soon as possible. They visited; Paul and Tom brought them up. Dr.

Akshadha never left; he was on the phone constantly. After the kids left and about another hour later, he came in and said someone else had some ideas. He doesn't work here and was not on call; however, he was on his way. His name is Dr. Shepard. Later that night he showed up, and Dr. Akshadha informed us that Dr. Shepard had had a stroke himself, to be aware of his disabilities. You know us; we judge no one. I said, no worries; anyone who can help!

At this point, we had tried getting flights for our mothers from where they were because they were stuck in severe storms in Alabama. The civilians from Alabama were all ready to pay for the flight; however, where they were, it just wasn't possible. Fionna [my manager from Alabama] also had called and said she was not waiting anymore, that she was on her way (from Alabama to California) Friday. She said Roxy and Nancy [friends/coworkers from Alabama] would be there the next day.

When I got off the phone, Dr. Shepard showed up and was reviewing your test results. He immediately wanted to try an aggressive treatment, because he was not satisfied this was it. He laid you flat in the bed and increased your blood pressure to 180. Within ten minutes, there was movement in your body. He changed the blood thinner type to an IV; that way it could be stopped tomorrow to do a procedure where they put a probe in your artery to see exactly what the damage is. He had warned me that this was all risky, and I had to sign a lot of consents, but my judgment said it was all worth it. He said that now you might survive but be paralyzed, but if this worked, then maybe not. He also said that if you were lying down, you would more than likely have trouble breathing and would have to be put on a ventilator, at which time you would be put into an induced coma.

I explained all this to you, and we went along with the plan. Dr. Shepard himself would do the procedure with the probe the next day. I insisted I would stay through the night with you, and the doctors agreed. Around midnight, I was sleeping when Dad woke me up because you had been having problems breathing. We told the nurses, and they agreed to call Dr. Akshadha. I talked you through that. You were about to be put to sleep, and when you woke up, you would have a tube in your mouth, down your throat, breathing for you. Ten minutes later, Dr. Akshadha was there and the procedure went fine. He drained a little bit of fluid from your lungs and had it sent for testing. At this point, he said you were now in a controlled environment and that I should go home. The kids stayed overnight at Diane's. Jasmyne [our pit bull] slept in bed with me, and I cried pretty much all night long. I was so scared!

12 December

Today was the day we were going to find out exactly what happened. Fionna showed around noon. Your mom and mine showed around nine or ten in the morning. Right as your mom showed up, they were putting in your two central lines, which would get rid of a bunch of the IVs in your arms. Anytime they did anything to you or found anything new, I would tell you several times so maybe it wouldn't be quite as scary. Around noon or 1:00 p.m., they did the procedure. It took about an hour or so. You did amazing, your vitals staying solid throughout all the moving around. About fifteen minutes later, Dr. Shepard came down and brought the pictures of what he found. He said it doesn't look good. You have a dissection in your artery where your neck meets the brain, another dissection in the left lobe of your brain, and a full clot above your right collarbone. He said there is nothing they can do with the clot, because it is too late, and if they did a clot buster, it could cause the two dissections to bleed out, which would kill you. However, as strange, rare, and bad as the two dissections looked, there was back flow (blood flow), which meant room for healing and room for recovery—potentially full recovery, he said. You were still critical, but the fact that there is hope is *great news*! He still was dumbfounded about how all this happened—not just one rare dissection but two.

I have never prayed so much as I have in the past few days, and I have even more of a reason to pray harder. Dr. Shepard also wanted you to be transferred to his hospital as soon as you were stable enough, so he could monitor you every day. Through this whole process—I know I haven't mentioned it until now—everyone has been great. The navy, friends, family, people we don't even know, nurses, doctors, social workers— everyone. Everyone is focusing on you and doing everything in their power. Grandma and Grandpa are attempting to relearn their roles of helping raise two little ones. Dad has a newfound respect for all you do on a day-to-day basis. Jasmyne is getting worse. I think it's because neither of us have been home, and she's freaking out a little bit. All in all it was a positive day.

13 December

This morning Dad, Paul, Diane, Tom, and family took the kids to the command Christmas party. They took lots of pictures. The kids had a blast. Noah still doesn't like Santa, and Emma was passed from mom to mom.

You had a pretty good morning. No setbacks, and in fact, things were looking like they were going to be able to transfer you to the hospital this weekend. The only thing they wanted to do first was put a stomach tube in to eventually see how your stomach was working and start feeding you in there instead of through the IV. At lunch, Fionna and I went home to spend some time with the kids, at which time she got some two hundred pictures of Noah and me. I hope some come out. When we got back, they said they wanted to hold off on the stomach tube until tomorrow. Around midday, you took a turn for the worse. Your heart rate skyrocketed, and your blood pressure fell way down. You could tell something was very wrong. You started dumping large amounts of fluids. Dr. Akshadha came in and said the part of your brain that controls general fluid retaining and preventing pumping of fluids or dehydration was affected by your strokes, so they gave you medicine so they could control it, and about an hour later you stabilized back to where you were. Because of what had just happened, they were no longer comfortable moving you to the other hospital this weekend.

Later that night Roxy and Nancy showed up, but it was right at shift change, so they had to wait until after to see you. Also Jessica showed up kind of unannounced. By now it was your mom and me, plus the three of them, and given what had happened earlier, the nurses were not happy with everyone being there. I didn't blame them. You stayed calm, and we left you be for the night.

14 December

Today when I had come back in, you had stayed stable through the night. They had come in to stop your blood thinner so they could put the tube in your stomach. Today I also brought the laptop in so I could go through the Christmas party pictures with you. It was emotional; we ended up having to stop because it was hard for you to hear the stories. They decided to postpone your transfer to the other hospital because of the stomach tube. They wanted to make sure nothing went wrong and that it would go smoothly.

Now I'm not sure whether to write it in today's block or tomorrow's, so I'm going to split it up. Pretty much most of the day I have had diarrhea and stomach pain; up until this point I had not been eating much or really having regular sleep. I knew I had been under a lot of stress, taking care of the kids and coming back to the hospital. By the time I got home that night, it seemed to have gotten worse. I lay on the couch, and Mom, Dad, Roxy, Nancy—everyone—was asking if I was okay. Of course I just said yes and went about my business.

15 December

Last night around 11:00 p.m. or so, I knew something was wrong. Dad kept saying that I was under a lot of stress, that was all, or maybe it was an ulcer. But like I've been telling you, we know our own bodies better than anyone else, and I knew something was wrong. So finally around 11:30 p.m., I told Dad I need to go to the ER to get checked out. We sat in the waiting area for about twenty minutes or so before I was finally admitted. I found out that it was Dr. Rodriguez, the same doctor you had that first day. I asked for another, but there were none. Long story short, I guess he heard who I was. I don't know if he was trying to kiss up or what, but they did X-rays and CT scans, took a stool sample and a urine sample, did blood work, all kinds of stuff. Well, around 6:30 a.m., they finally discharged me with all kinds of meds.

Unfortunately, it is contagious. Come to find out, Mom, both kids, Roxy, and Nancy all had it too. So we were all laid up in bed and in pain, and today is the day you're transferring hospitals, so we needed to be there also. Ah! Always five things going at once! I slept it off for a few hours and was able to suck it up to get to the hospital just as they were loading you into the ambulance. I had the kids because everyone at home was too sick to take care of them. Dad drove Roxy, I drove your mom, and we met the ambulance at the new hospital.

The staff over here is very friendly and professional, and immediately got you all set up. The transfer was a success! Later I picked up food, drinks, and meds for the girls, and they called all upset from the hotel because they came down to help and here I was, taking care of them. It's no big deal. That's what we do, right, babe?

16 December

First night at the new hospital! It didn't go badly. They have been trying to set up a time to take the tube in your mouth out and put a trachea in. They set up a time for tomorrow, and we were doing all the tests required for it when they found that your blood count was low. They wanted to do a blood transfusion over the night. So I spent today talking you through the steps of what they were going to do, like I have for all the procedures to date. Overall you pretty much just slept today and caught up on your rest.

17 December

I walked in this morning to you looking different. Something was just not right. You had gotten your transfusion last night. They said all went well, but you were coughing *a lot.* They sedated you more, but it still did not look or sound good. They began suctioning you and getting a lot of clear liquid out. I could tell this was making the nurses nervous. I stayed calm in front of you, telling you we could get through this and to fight whatever it was. Well, it turned out your lungs were filling up with fluid—something called pulmonary edema. There wasn't much we could do because of your situation; we had to just wait it out and hope it dried out. Everything you had been weaned off of last night medical-wise had to be restarted to keep you calm and free of pain as much as possible. Because of this, they also canceled your trachea surgery for the day and rescheduled it for tomorrow, assuming this gets better. They put you on more antibiotics, and we were back to the waiting game.

18 December

Well, your lungs have cleared and you're back on the forward path, which is good news. They stopped your blood thinner today so they can put the trachea in and get that tube out of your mouth. The doctor doing it is kind of old; in fact, when he first gave us the procedure description, I thought he was another patient from the hospital who was lost! It was funny. I'll tell you more about it later. Anyhow, so I just walked you through what they were going to do so that when you woke up, you wouldn't freak out, and to tell you that this was a big step toward the right direction. Well, of course you pulled through; all went well with the procedure. In fact, you looked *beautiful*! Seeing you without that tube in your mouth, no tape around your face … You looked so much more at ease and comfortable. You were in quite a bit of pain, but that was to be expected because of the fresh incision. But overall it was a great day!

22 December

This morning was a rough morning. Dr. Akshadha had wanted to talk to me about different treatments, and when I came in, he was in there too. He asked me to step out with him to talk as he usually does. However, it was all right next to you for you to hear it all. He said that if you stop improving or don't improve, maybe we should research stem cell development. It's illegal in the States as far as I know, and it has never been tested on humans, only animals. So obviously, there's an extreme risk. Now, I know we talked, and I know you don't want to live as a locked-in quadriplegic, and if time told you that you would never get better, then we have nothing to lose. However, you have been improving by great strides, so I told him we'll take it day by day but are *not* going into research yet!

Well, you had heard everything, and it made you very

emotional and sad. I tried to calm you, but it just seemed as if you wanted to give up after that. About an hour later, we were telling stories and I mentioned your making your johnnycake. Toward the end of the story, you broke out with this huge, full-face smile! It about brought everyone to tears. Your mom got so excited, she went and got a nurse, who immediately came and saw, just to have an even bigger smile on her face. Your mom started pacing the room, so I told her to go the waiting room and start calling everyone (I know that's what she wanted to do). It was truly good news. This completely changed the mood of the day!

That's where the journal ended. I realize there are three days missing—December 19, 20, and 21. I awoke from the coma on December 20. Then the real challenges began: recovery.

I don't really remember exactly "waking up," rather just being.

After a few days with the nurse I awoke to, I was transferred to another unit before being placed in ICU. My nurse was a sweet young woman by the name of Kathy. I remember waking and being with her a few nights. I didn't know hours. I only knew that dark equals sleep, turn off lights, night; days equals hustle bustle, turn on lights. I distinctly remember Kathy saying, "While I was in the mall last night, I came across these lip glosses in Victoria's Secret and thought of you. I didn't know what color you'd like, so I got all three. Do you like pink?" Then she looked into my eyes, not waiting for a response, and sweetly continued, "Pink goes best with your complexion. Yeah, I bet you like pink. Pink it is."

Chapter 7

The Shadows of Death

What the journal doesn't talk about are the experiences I had while in the coma, while I was circling the drain off and on. I know just how off the wall this sounds; I know things I shouldn't know about people who visited, sheer peace, and a knowing that I was never alone.

First I was in my bed, one of my best friends from California Aubree was by the left side, holding my hand, caressing it, just carrying on a conversation like we were talking on the phone. It was as if I was looking down on the room. I could see everyone who was in my room. I could hear the conversations play out as Jackson stood at the foot of my bed, on the left, talking to Bailey, another one of my best friends from California, who was standing next to him, on my right, drinking a cup of coffee. That actually happened. It would later be confirmed not only by Jackson but by the people involved: the layout of people, the conversations, and all.

Next, Jackson and I were by our hot tub, hanging out on our back porch. It was really hazy, and I couldn't breathe. He kept telling me, "Hang in there, Peyton. Everything's going to be all right." He had his arm wrapped around me. My body was on fire and was severely itchy. Next thing I knew, Dr. Akshadha was kneeling in front of me, saying, "Everything's going to be okay." I saw him; Akshadha was my doctor! I knew who he was before I was told, for one. And two, I have a tracheotomy scar from where he inserted the trachea in my neck so I was able to breathe. Without the trachea, I would have died. I believe it was the beginning of going into shock, my mind's way of dealing with the situation at hand. I don't believe in coincidences.

Next is the strangest memory by far. I was in a large room, like a lobby, with a handful of others. I was sitting on a yoga mat when a nurse came over and said to me and another girl, "Whoever swallows this banana can stay. But the one that doesn't has to leave." What in the heck, I have this thing in my neck. I don't know how, but surely if you show me, show me just once, I know I can figure it out. Tough luck. She wouldn't show me and the other girls already swallowed her banana. "Here, this will help you let go, help to calm you." She put these things on my arms and legs that were tight, constricting; they looked like leg warmers from the eighties. So I walked out the front door and hopped into our truck. Jackson was driving. He said, "How'd it go?"

"Not good," I said, "but they gave me these to help me let go," and I showed him the warmers. "It's okay, I can go now. I'm okay with it."

"I don't think so." He ripped them off and was on the phone to my friend Roxy. She met us at a hotel with an ambulance, where the EMT loaded me onto a stretcher and put an oxygen mask on me. Jackson wouldn't let them take me to the hospital for hours—weird, right? I believe that by ripping those warmers off me, Jackson saved my life.

I believe this one happened as I was being transferred to the new hospital. You'll see why. I was in the back of an ambulance. During the whole ride, a brown wooden coffin kept slamming into my gurney. We got to the hospital, where my friends and family (Roxy, Nancy, Fionna, Mom, and Jackson) were awaiting my arrival. They took me inside. The hallway lights were bright. Then I was in a room with Jackson and the kids, well aware that I was sitting hunched over, with no strength. I was unable to move anything, and all I wanted to do was hold my baby. I knew I couldn't function, that something was wrong. They *were* there when I got transferred, those people—in the hospital parking lot when the ambulance came in. How'd I know that? I was barely stable enough for the transfer to take place.

Next I was lying in my bed in the ICU, and Roxy and Nancy were leaving to go home to Alabama; they were at the head of my bed with Jackson. Roxy leaned in and gave my forehead a kiss and said how much she loved me and that she would see me later. Then I wasn't alone in my bed. My good friend from high school was there wearing a blue sweater, and I was grasping her cold hand. She had died a few years back. She was just lying next to me as she had when she was lying in the coffin. I was really scared; I didn't want them to go. I was screaming and sobbing, but they couldn't hear. I was holding her cold hand ever so tightly.

The part about Roxy and Nancy leaving and where they were standing and Roxy kissing my forehead was later confirmed; it happened just as I said. I also knew they had gotten the stomach bug while here and saw Roxy drop to her knees, curling up on the floor of my hospital room because of it. Spine chilling, huh?

Next I was standing in a hospital room, like a surgical operating room that I always see on *Grey's Anatomy* (my favorite TV show). There was a metal table in front of me. I was wearing a gown and an oxygen mask. I was weak. The side door opened, and I stumbled out it. Then once I got out, I was running in this beautiful meadow with grass up to my outstretched hands, sunshine gleaming on my face, the warm breeze gently blowing. I got a little ways, and then I heard a deep male voice saying, "Peyton, what about Noah? He needs you," so I reluctantly turned around and went back through the doors.

Last, there was a young girl with curly brown hair, in a blue dress, kneeling and praying at the windowsill of my room.

There also was a tall, skinny man, dressed all in white, sitting at the left end of my bed, by my feet, reading a newspaper, never letting me see his face. I would scream at them, "I'm not going with you. You can't take me." They weren't there to take me; I believe they were there to help me, to help harness all of the prayers being said for me around the world. I have always described the man as a younger version of my dad. I believe that's just who it was. And after reading the book "Heaven is for Real" by Todd Burpo in which his son Colton has some similar experiences I'm convinced.

I told Jackson about them, but he said my room was empty. He never saw my visions but can attest to the fact that some did occur or are linked to what occurred. They may have happened simultaneously; they may have been days apart. I kind of lost track of time. I believe they were more than mere visions. I believe the confirmed happenings were walking through the valley of the shadow of death and looking down on my body and the actual occurrences taking place, seeing the people involved, feeling the affection of my loved ones willing me to return. The others, I believe, were my mind struggling to come to terms with coming back. You make your own conclusions. As for me, I don't believe in coincidences.

Chapter 8

Blink Once for Yes

I woke from the coma peacefully, not freaking out but knowing I was locked in, knowing I could communicate only with Jackson. We spent the day I woke trying to discern an easier way to communicate, because my doctors said that my blinks couldn't be trusted.

Jackson went to the store and got all these refrigerator magnets and a magnetic board. Then, as he was setting them up into words and moving them around, he realized that I wouldn't be able to use them. I had no way to push them about the board. I was paralyzed, God love him.

We settled on this communication board he picked up at Walgreens. It had *A–E, F–J, K–O, P–T, U–Y,* and *Z.* The doctors said my blinks couldn't be trusted, but Jackson had faith. He believed I could blink once for yes and squeeze my eyes shut for no.

Jackson was the only one who could use this system to communicate with me. The doctors or nurses wouldn't even try, not believing that I was really communicating with him at all. He got so good, he didn't even need it. He'd say, "Column one, two, three, four; row one, two," and so on. He'd stop where I blinked my eyes. I only had to give him a word and he'd have my whole sentence—thankfully, because that was tedious! It was like we were on the same wavelength. He got to where he could read the most minimal expression on my face.

Dr. Shepard was the only doctor who would give me any

sort of credit for being alive within my shell. The doctor walked with a limp. He himself had suffered a stroke a few years back. He assured us it was going to be a long road, and that although I might not recover fully, he had faith. He knew Jackson wasn't making it up. He believed I was in there.

When I woke from the coma, it was a surprise to everyone that I could smile. It was completely involuntary and had to be provoked, but it was an ear-to-ear grin just the same. When I gave my first smile, Jackson and my mom were of course in the room, along with my ICU nurse and the blond-haired, first-year resident who took the time to save my life, was standing in the door way.

During the first month in the hospital in California, I was in excruciating pain in the back of my head, where the dissections were. It *hurt*. I begged Jackson every day for a month to smother me. I had no hope; I saw no silver lining. Can you honestly picture the once very active me like this *forever*? He refused to listen to such ranting. He would simply turn away until I was finished. I was screaming inside. Imagine being able to communicate only by blinking *if* the person looks at you, and having that person end the conversation, refusing to let you speak, and turn their back on you! *Super frustrating!*

Crying inside, absolutely falling apart at every seam, I can't describe to you the worthless, hopeless feelings of trying to come to terms with being told I'd be like this, useless, at twenty-seven—trapped forever in my body, a body that felt as heavy as concrete. I would never again hold my children, play, laugh, or even move. It just wasn't acceptable.

During my stay in California, Jackson knew my charts and meds better than any of the nurses. He'd communicate anything and everything I had to say. He'd help them tube-feed me, suction my trachea, crush and distribute my meds, exercise my weakened, paralyzed limbs, change me, bathe me, and make sure they rotated morphine with something else every three hours because he was concerned about addiction. He even helped transfer me to the weekly CT scan. He slipped right into his nature, being in control of everything.

Because of all he knew and did, they thought he had had medical training. He knew more about my charts and meds and was better prepared than they were, and he did more.

Daily he would have me practice moving my eyebrows up and down, saying I needed to show the doctors they were wrong, that I was making progress. And every time I would start to "cry"—really, it was more like a moaning, wounded moose—he would say, "Raise your eyebrows," and I would spend so much energy concentrating on that task, I'd forget to continue to cry.

It felt good to move something and to prove Dr. Akshadha wrong. That sparked a little interest in me. We didn't give up. Jackson was beyond being my physical therapist; he was my inspirational motivator.

Then came sitting in a chair for at least four hours a day so my body wouldn't get used to only lying down. Oh how I hated that chair! Jackson, not the staff, would transfer me to a chair and strap me in for a few hours every day. When they transferred me, they'd use this belt, for safety, and every time, they'd have a hard time handling the dead weight and either pinch the trachea tube or pull the stomach tube or catheter. *Ouch.* Now imagine not being able to tell them, "Stop: you're hurting me!" and having to just wait until they figure it out.

The therapists there told us, "We just aren't prepared for you, a stroke victim; we deal mainly with heart attack victims. We're not set up for someone like you." A brain attack survivor—so it was really a learn-as-you-go process for us.

Jackson would be with me from eight in the morning until eight at night, flanked by my ever-loyal mother. They would break for an hour or two to go home and have lunch and comfort

Noah, who just didn't understand. He would stand by the door looking out the window, crying for hours on end with our pit bull, Jasmyne, by his side. When they'd finally come in, he'd make them immediately take their shoes off, for fear they were going to leave. Poor baby.

Jackson's mom and dad and my mom all took time off from work to come from Connecticut to California to help Jackson with the house and the kids; Jackson's mom took the entire year off so she could step in for me and care for the children, animals and house and allow Jackson to be at the hospital with me.

The navy was very supportive, helpful, and understanding. So was the community we had just moved into. Noah and Emma had the best Christmas ever. I hadn't had time to finish my Christmas shopping, or really even start, and the navy family realized that. We take care of our own—that's how they think. There was a mountain of gifts under that six-foot Christmas tree; people just kept dropping them by the house. And wouldn't you know, there wasn't a duplicate among them.

No one had to cook dinner for the next month because there were constantly homemade dinners, desserts, and fruit baskets being dropped off. I got to see a video of Noah lying in bed with Jackson late at night eating a yellow apple that was bigger than his head.

I am so very grateful to everyone who unselfishly pitched in and helped us out. You can't fathom my unwavering gratitude; I still, to this day, get choked up just thinking about it. It's a debt I can never repay.

When Jackson would leave at 8:00 p.m., I would make sure I got my much-needed morphine dose. I got morphine and something else, I can't remember what, every three hours for pain and by the two-and-a-half-hour mark, I was hurting bad and waiting, anxiously, for the next dose. It came as scheduled during the day—Jackson made sure of it—but at night, after he left, that was a totally different story. I would spend hours trying to get my male Jamaican night nurse to notice me and acknowledge me. I would stare at my communication board on the wall to my right, waiting for him to pick it up, but he never did.

After a few nights I learned that I could cry louder—moan, kind of—when I was in enough pain. Even that didn't get his attention. From a distance he would stare at me and say, "Are you hungry? I'm sorry, Mrs. Edwards; I don't know what you want." After watching the hours tick by, the curly-haired brunette RN, a sweet gal, would come in responding to my never-ending cries, look in my eyes, stroke my hair, and say, "Peyton, honey, are you in pain? Here, this ought to help you." *Finally*, relief. *And by the time my next one comes due,* I thought, *Jackson will be here.* He was my saving grace. I had that man on a pedestal no one could touch. I relied on him for everything, and he delivered.

Jackson was sure to keep me up with the current events happening not only locally, but around the world. It made me sad. I couldn't have cared less. It just reinforced the fact that I was going to be inside the four walls of this godforsaken room for who knew how long. I didn't want to see anyone, besides family, from the outside world or hear anything about it. Jackson didn't let me put that wall fully up that separated me from the outside world; he made sure to keep me current.

Dr. Akshadha wanted to put me in a nursing home, a halfway house thing where Jackson could come but the kids and pets couldn't. *Seriously.* Dr. Shepard was the only doctor who gave me any chance of recovery and believed I could do it. I believe that was in large part because he had suffered a stroke years before, and when he recovered, he specifically went into the stroke field to help other victims turn into survivors and recover. He was a sweet, gentle, modest, blond-haired man who walked with both of his knees bent in because of the stroke.

Not only did he survive, but look at him, a lead neurologist in the stroke field, post-stroke. It gave me hope, a spark of desire.

Jackson researched and researched, and found a hospital rehab right in Connecticut, just forty-five minutes to an hour away from where his parents lived. The lead neurologist was excited to take my case on, but TRICARE (military insurance) didn't want to cover the flight to get me there. Jackson took a step further; he wrote a letter to a congressman, who in turn very displeasingly called the secretary of the navy, who then called so on and so on, down the line.

Chapter 9

General Hospital

I was flown home, along with my mother, on a Friday in mid-February to General Rehabilitation Center in Connecticut in just three short hours, and the navy picked up the bill. I was so scared. There was a blizzard, and here they were, loading me, helpless and in pain, into an ambulance with blankets over my head and zooming me across town to my new home. All I could imagine was the worst. I thought I was never going to make it there alive. But through God's good grace, I did.

Dr. Michael Pierson, my father-in-law, and my aunt Shelby met us at the ER entrance, and I was taken to my new home for the next few months.

Upon my arrival, a nurse with curly brunette hair and wearing a blue winter coat gave me a hug and told a crying, frightened me, "Don't worry—you're going to be just fine. In two years I'm going to see you walking in Home Depot with a cane." I thought, *what an awful, wretched, mean thing to say. Do you not see me? Have you not heard of my hopeless case? Do you not know they expect no improvement and I have a husband and two small kids at home! How dare you!*

My mom stayed the night with me because I was terrified and they didn't know how to communicate with me. Neither did my mom yet, but she had seen Jackson do it multiple times. She stayed pretty much the whole week. Within that first hour I had her ask for morphine because I was in pain. An older, curly-haired, blonde nurse ever so politely replied, "We don't do

intravenous drugs on this floor. I'll go grab you some Tylenol 3."
I'm sorry, *what?* I had had morphine three hours earlier, and now
this stupid, mean, blonde nurse wanted to give me bleepety-
bleep-beep-bleep Tylenol? *Are you bleepin' kidding me?* Perfect. Just
perfect. It took a week or so for my body to adjust to this new
pain medicine and accept it. Until it did, I was in near-constant
pain at the bottom of the back of my neck where the brain-stem
stroke occurred. You see, they couldn't go in and surgically fix
the dissected veins; I'd die immediately, so they had to let the
dissections heal themselves, at their own pace.

Within four days this crazy new doctor was taking my
trachea out. I was scared out of my mind. *What if he takes it out
and my body doesn't remember how to breathe? Jackson and my kids
are making the long haul from California, and oh my heavens to Betsy,
I'm going to die! I'm going to die without saying good-bye. My kids will
never have the opportunity to know me and know how much I loved
them.* I was so afraid; I was frantic, thinking of my funeral and
all they'd say, never seeing my babies grow up and get married.
I begged my mom not to leave me. I was so afraid to be alone in
this new strange, uncomfortable place. The nurses put a cot for
my mom on my right, next to my bed. I was in my own room,
because my case was so unique. They'd never seen a locked-in
quadriplegic, especially such a young one.

My nurses were allowed to care for me and me alone; because
I needed so much supervision and tending to, they were allowed
to be responsible only for me. My room was literally ten feet
from the nurses' station. I didn't find that comforting, by the
way—more like mortifying. I mean, if you're set right next to
the nurses, it can't be good.

To comfort me, my family came up with a clever idea to help
ease the pain of being away from my loved ones and to help
motivate me. It was meant to remind me why I couldn't give in
and just fall into the black hole that was closing in around me,

ready to cave in at any moment. It was meant to remind me I was someone's wife, mother, daughter, cousin, and friend.

They covered four huge, white poster boards with pictures of my friends and my son, baby girl, husband, and me before the stroke. They hung them in my room toward the left side of my bed, in front of the curtains I would never allow anyone to open because seeing the outside made me sad and then quickly devastated. The nurses, doctors, and CNAs had never seen anything like it. Jackson's dad and my mom had set up one of those rolling tables at the foot of my bed covered with pictures and cards the night I arrived.

For a while it made the darkness creep in more. I would stare at it at night and just sob. I missed my husband, my kids. Missed holding my baby girl, feeding her, changing her, snuggling with her and Noah. I was alone, alone with my thoughts, forced to learn patience and choose my words wisely, because spelling words, let alone sentences, was not only tedious but exhausting.

Jackson called from California to have a phone conference in my room with Dr. Pierce the first week I was there before making the four day trek to Connecticut. At first I was ecstatic to hear his voice, and then, just like that, I was bawling hysterically. I couldn't stop, couldn't control it; I felt the hopelessness sweep over me, and then unbelievable sadness and pain. They had to move the conference call to an office down the hall, where Dr. Pierce said the inappropriate fluctuations of happiness, sadness, anger, and crying were not only expected but perfectly normal. I had to retrain not only the muscles in my body but also the one known as the brain.

The brain stem controls everything in your body—your movement, thinking, feeling, swallowing, cognitive reasoning, eye movement and emotions. I had a brain-stem dissection, a blood clot and a left side dissection, I should be dead. No doctor can believe I'm alive, let alone tell me why my brain had a severe brain attack or why I survived. I was a medical mystery. I needed to rewire my brain, which was currently wildly hysterical.

I came in on a Friday, and on Monday morning I met my therapists. I was getting physical therapy, occupational therapy, and speech therapy, although I couldn't do OT and speech yet, since my jaw was locked tighter than Fort Knox. It wouldn't open for anything. I couldn't even move my tongue. Every now and then, it would release to yawn involuntarily, but I couldn't control it. I might smile from ear to ear, but not if I tried to do it. It had to be provoked, which wasn't hard, because when I was in the coma, they put me on a bunch of antidepressants, fearing that my mind was so jumbled, I wouldn't understand and would get frantic and give myself a heart attack. I was either extremely happy or devastatingly sad. There was no happy medium. And my hands were clenched into tight fists when they weren't forced open to be in the on-again, off-again plastic braces every four hours. It was lovely.

Do you realize how much you move each day? How many skin cells you shed by moving, twitching, rubbing? I couldn't move, so I shed none, but that doesn't mean I didn't grow new ones. My mom would peel long, outlining layers off my hands and feet. I like to peel burnt skin off a back as much as the next guy, but this was thick and somewhat attached. I was shedding like a snake skin. It was gross.

I was very emotionally unstable. I was happy at times only because of the amount of antidepressants I was on. I spent my evenings alone, and that's when the walls would close in and the floor would cave. I would cry a lot—if that's what you would call the moaning noise my mouth would release—between the pain in the lower back side of my head and missing my family. I yearned for them.

I was ashamed, humiliated, embarrassed, and just plain devastated that I was twenty-seven years old, by far the youngest patient on this floor by fifty years and forced to rely on others for everything; I had never felt so useless and worthless. Thank God for antidepressants that would let me sink for only a short time. My involuntary spastic emotions worked to my advantage, because all anyone had to do was smile, and regardless of how upset I was, I would smile back.

I had just had a baby and didn't get to hold, dress, feed, and snuggle her. I was deathly afraid that she wouldn't know who I was. And Noah, my sweet, sweet boy, was afraid of me. I thought for sure he would forget me; the thought devastated me.

Jackson knew this bothered me and said he wouldn't let either of them forget me. He would bring them in once a week for a half hour or forty-five minutes, but it was more uncomfortable and stressful than anything else.

He would put baby Emma on my chest so she could hold her dinner bottle and drink it. By now she was seven months old. He wanted it to be a bonding experience. As sweet of a gesture as it was, it made me more paranoid and uncomfortable than anything.

The bed had rails, of course, one at my head and one at my feet, and then at each side, the combined length of the bed. But what if she pulled a wrong piece of tubing or rolled and no one saw her and she fell? As soon as she finished that bottle, she wanted nothing to do with me and would crawl on the bed to reach for the person closest to her. I was so sad but relieved.

I was anxious and uncomfortable the entire time, and Noah, my sweet little mama's boy wouldn't come near me. He avoided me like the plague—wouldn't even glance in my direction. It broke my heart that he didn't want me, that he was afraid. I was sure he had forgotten me and didn't know me. And I couldn't reach out to comfort him or at least talk and let him know everything was okay. I had no way to soothe his fears, but was forced to just sit and watch as they devoured us both. I loved seeing them, but their visits made me so very sad.

Jackson and the kids were staying with Jackson's mom and dad, forty-five minutes away. The whole reason we had chosen this facility was to have a place to stay that would be relatively close. They began remodeling the unfinished basement in anticipation of my being allowed to come home eventually. Jackson and his dad worked hard painting the walls and carpeting the concrete floors. They hired contractors to rework the backyard landscaping and add a long concrete ramp to the basement entrance. They also added a black removable ramp to the upstairs front door of the house so I wouldn't be confined to just one area inside the house. That way I would feel as much at home as possible and could even go outside and watch the children play. They had the downstairs bathroom completely remodeled so that it would be easily accessible for the wheelchair there was no doubt I would need. Jackson would accept no other alternative besides the fact that I was going to get better and come home to my family once again. They worked hard turning the basement into a home where I could feel comfortable, whether inside or out.

Jackson would make the forty-five-minute commute every day, to help with physical therapy, encourage me, be there when it got to be too much and I'd fall to pieces, and sometimes just to visit. He was very much involved in my recovery process, knowing the ins and outs of everything. There were some days I got caught in the deep, dark hole and was so sad, he made the commute twice in the same day. It didn't happen often, but when it did, it was horrible.

As a general rule, Jackson or my mother was always by my side. The pedestal I had Jackson on kept growing higher and higher. He was God in my eyes. I was ever so grateful of him. On the other hand, I thought it was my mom's "duty" to be there.

My appreciation for her and the realization of what she did for me didn't come until much later—years later, actually.

I had a PEG tube for bowl-less feeding and a catheter for urine outtake, of course. They were *always* in the way, getting pulled or caught on the Hoyer net they would use to transfer me. They didn't use a belt like in California; they used a net that caught me like a fish and moved me to the chair—not so fun. My eyes would widen in a gasp of pain, and the nurses would realize eventually and apologize and quickly work to remedy it.

I had to go to bowl-less feeding so I wouldn't be overfed. Jackson had demanded this because a few times when I was in California, the nurses would start feeding me and give me too much. I'd be full but had no way to convey it when Jackson wasn't there, and I would start vomiting it back up. The nurses back in California wouldn't take the time to learn to use the letter board to communicate with me. I don't like vomiting under normal circumstances, much less while lying down. Vomiting while completely paralyzed was even worse.

I was uncomfortable around anyone but Jackson and my newfound hospital family of trained professionals. From Jackson I drew the strength and courage to continue, and those pictures on the board reminded me of just what I was fighting for. Regardless, I never saw an end in sight, never a light at the end of the tunnel. I saw no silver lining.

Dr. Pierce would see me every morning for 8:00 a.m. rounds. He was a brilliant, tall, older, balding man with a very dry sense of humor, so I was told by his colleagues. I loved him. I began to not only feel comfortable with him, but to really like him, and I found him to be quite hilarious actually. My nurses, CNAs, and therapists thought I was crazy. I thought he was fantastic. When no one else but family and one California doctor had the slightest faith in me, he did. He noticed all my "little" improvements and knew they were big. I have the greatest respect and highest admiration for him. I was allowed to be in rehab for only thirty days; however, he kept me there for three months, because he kept seeing improvements along with my growing desire to get better.

On one of my first afternoons, a young girl came in to get permission to see me and help out on my case. She was a student who would be working with Rachael, my Occupational Therapist. Every now and then she would be accompanying Rachael and shadowing her, but she had to get my permission first. My mom was with me, and after she left, I communicated with her, "I know her; I worked with her. Her name is Allie Alexander." My mom bolted out of the room after her and said, "Is your name Allie Alexander? My daughter knows you." A shocked Allie came back in the room and really observed me. Then I smiled at her and she said, "Oh my goodness! Peyton! I'm so sorry this happened to you! I love you!" She came back later in the week with a card and a little yellow plaque that is now in my living room that reads, "She believed she could so she did." She immediately had unyielding faith that I would not only survive but fully recover. I couldn't believe I'd been away from Connecticut for years, came back broken in more ways than one, and lo and behold, I knew someone at this hospital. Wicked. I still keep in contact with her today.

Chapter 10

Physical and Occupational Therapy

That first Monday, my occupational and physical therapists walked in, and the work immediately began. The very first thing they made me do was sit up on the edge of my bed. Sounds easy enough, right? Wrong!

The two girls (Mary Katherine, my physical therapist, and Rachael, my occupational therapist) would get one in front and one behind and hoist me up and sling my legs around the right side of the bed. I have no muscles; the ones I worked so hard to gain have atrophied and disappeared. I sat on the edge of the bed for five minutes, the longest five minutes ever, completely slumped. I had no core muscles, my head was down, and I looked up, my neck wobbling like a newborn baby with an unsupported head, unable to move any other muscle.

I felt helpless, scared that I was going to fall face first on the hard, cold, tiled floor. They never would have let me, but that didn't comfort me. I wasn't thinking about that. I was thinking, *They'll look away for the slightest moment and I'll fall, and along with being paralyzed I'll have a broken arm, leg, or skull, and what if, what if, what if.* I had to be watched like a newborn baby.

We did this for a few days (it felt like forever); we had to strengthen core muscles before we could start on anything else. I would hear them coming and cringe. I hated to hear them come, because it reminded me of just how much I had lost, and the hopelessness of the long, winding road that lay ahead, and the pain. I would not only hurt at the base of my head, but I'd feel that soreness you get when you attempt to work out after a few years of not doing it. I knew I was about to hurt.

After a few days of that, they put a stack of pillows on each side of me and had me lean down to the right, pull up straight, and then lean down to the left and pull up straight. Doesn't sound that hard, right? Wrong. It was scary, because I didn't have hands that could reach out and catch me, protecting me from falling. My brain was being rewired. They had to tell me what they wanted me to do as well as demonstrate; then I would happily oblige. I was eager to get moving and learn how. I literally started the exercise falling: they would sit one on each side and help me down and up, getting my core muscles as well as brain waves used to exercise again.

After a few weeks off the morphine, which made me tired and even weaker, my muscles started to wake; I started some "minor" movement. I could tap my left index finger. It was the only movement I had, so I did it constantly. I was elated.

Within the next two weeks, I became able to move my left pointer finger and my left thumb. Mary Katherine and Rachael continued to come by my room and exercise my legs and arms in my bed. They became my friends; they were such sweet women, and funny! Pretty soon I no longer cringed when I'd hear them coming. I became extremely comfortable with them; I'd see them once in the morning and again in the afternoon after break, lunch, and nap. Minimal movement tired me out, and I wasn't even the one doing it!

Movement came back gradually, after the first two fingers; I was able to move all the fingers on my left hand. Fancy that: I'm right-handed. And Rachael went to work prying the fingers on my right hand open and stretching and bending them. Then it went to trying to turn my head. Yes and no, up and down. It would get stuck a lot, and the nurses would have to come reposition it for me. It was really slow moving, and painful when it got stuck, but I'd get so exciting doing it. Then I became able to lift my left forearm, although with no control; it was very wobbly. My day nurse gave me a washcloth to wash my face; I had to move my head and hand in sync. I was like a kid on Christmas morning! I used the same technique to apply my lip balm. It gave Rachael a little more range of motion to work with. She knew my stopping point, because it would start to be tight and resistant and didn't want to go any farther.

One night Jackson walked in, and I picked up my weak and wobbly forearm with no control and waved to him. I clenched my fingers to the palm of my hand and released and extended them. I was like a baby learning to wave. He was shocked and ecstatic. He couldn't believe it. He called family immediately to share the good news. I was excited and giddy about my newfound talent so I tried it out on my nightly bloodsucker after she drew my blood. She stood by the door getting ready to turn off the light and say bye when I lifted my forearm, weakly and wobbly, and waved. She shut off the light, quickly turned it on, and exclaimed, "Oh my goodness! Did you just wave to me? You just waved to me!" She was so excited, she cried! She would talk to me every night when she came in to get blood from me; she was such a sweet lady. My nurses and therapists and CNAs noticed all of my little improvements because they worked so closely with me on a daily basis. The joy and enthusiasm spread like a wildfire. I keep in contact with many of them to this day. They will hold a very, very special place in my heart forever.

At first there was nothing for the Occupational Therapist to work with, because my hands were clenched into tight fists that she could barely pry open, even using all her strength. The harder she tried, the more my fingers dug into my palm, which didn't allow her to do anything. So she assisted the physical therapist in manually exercising my arms and legs, not wanting the limbs to forget completely how to work and be rendered useless.

Mary Katherine would bend my legs up and then straighten them out. My right leg felt like it was concrete, it was so, so heavy. While she was doing that, Rachael would help my elbows bend in and out and my arms go up and down. She had to move them slowly, because my muscles and joints had atrophied and weren't very flexible in their range of motion. My range was pretty much nonexistent. It felt like my arms had just ... seized up. There was no lifting them up, no rotation, and certainly no range of motion.

Chapter 11

Speech

After the girls were finished with their form of torture, it was time for Richard, my speech therapist. I would see Richard twice a day every day, after physical and occupational therapies every morning and afternoon. He is the sweetest guy, and an avid bird-watcher. He was great; he started out by writing notes and goals on the whiteboard in front of me to my right, because my mouth was still clamped shut and unable to be worked with. I was afraid to tell anyone that the writing on the whiteboard was in double vision and shadowed for the first two weeks I was there. I was afraid of what that might mean. I had had enough bad news; I couldn't handle any more.

I want you to think, for just a second, of the sound of your own voice and the various ways in which you use it—for example, showing excitement, being stern and authoritative—and the power of using that "mom voice" when needed. You probably have never even given it any thought. I know I sure didn't. It is just something most of us have done naturally since we were little. It is effortless and easy: as with the ability to blink or breathe or walk, there's no need to think about it; you just do it. That is, until it's no longer an option. Then it becomes a whole different ball game.

In the brain, speaking is a complex process involving many parts working in cooperation and communicating efficiently that comes from the brain stem. An interruption in any part of this process—say, a dissection of the basil artery-controlling motor functions—can result in challenging communication.

Think about it. Your voice is a very fundamental part of who you are, just like your height or hair color. Jackson's commanding, baritone voice yields a very different impression than my slurred weak voice. I no longer had a "mom voice" or a "me voice," just this weak, moaning voice. I could and can easily be spoken over.

Even if it's done only subconsciously, different perceptions are formed in the person speaking as well as in the person hearing the speech. We place value on the sound of our own voices. Your speech affects who you are as a person, no matter how much you want to believe it doesn't. Not being able to speak "properly" creates a distance, a divide between you and others and a separation from the human mainstream. It keeps you away from the "normies" and not really wanting to converse with the general public. It makes you choose what words you do say very, very carefully, and to speak the very least amount needed to get your point across. People have little patience for my speaking difficulties, and I have even less with them, or should I say with their impatience with me. I have none with myself. It's very frustrating. I work very hard at changing my perspective on that.

Richard's long-term goal was for me to leave talking and swallowing without being a danger to myself. I couldn't go home if I was a swallowing risk. I needed to be able to nourish myself without the help of regular tube feedings to supplement. I thought it to be a tall order to fill, but I was ready to start and give it my all. I desperately wanted to go home to my family, to my babies.

After the first month at General, I could open my mouth ever so slightly. And when I say slightly, I mean maybe an inch. Richard began work right away. We had to start with the very basics—oo, ee, ah—exaggerating the facial expressions while trying to open the mouth farther.

After I got the initial vowel sounds down, we moved on to work on proper tongue placement to create the sounds of each letter of the alphabet. For instance, he couldn't simply say, "What does *N* say?" He had to say, "Put your tongue at the roof of your mouth behind your teeth and make the *n* sound." And then he would have to demonstrate. That's the way my brain seemed to rewire. First he told me how, and then he demonstrated and explained how to mirror his movements. I needed this to comprehend every step, no matter how simple. Without it, my brain just didn't understand. Then we would move on to single-syllable words. He would give me sheets to practice on my own as nightly "homework."

Richard wanted to see if my vocal cords were damaged when they put the tracheotomy tube in, so he called his colleague at Memorial to bring a specialized machine to look. This machine was attached to a long, thin, black rubber hose with a camera in it that they shoved up my nose to get a better look at my throat. His colleague started the procedure, but we had to stop it and restart it because it was so uncomfortable. I had lost the ability to control my body and emotions and just sit there, tolerate it, and remain still.

My vocal cords weren't damaged, so that was good, right? Right. Turns out my soft palate was paralyzed, which makes my speech sound nasally, and if I'm not careful when I'm drinking—if I'm not sitting up straight or with my head slightly tilted back—the fluid will come out my nose. That is not very pleasant.

The soft palate is a valve that closes off air to your nose. When the soft palate is not working properly, air comes out your nose. For example, if you say "ed" repeatedly, it sounds like "n." With *b* words such as *web, crib,* and so on, the *b* will sound like "m." I have called my son Noah Bubbie since he was a baby; it now sounds like "mummy." If I squeeze my nostrils shut while saying "Bubbie," I stop them from releasing air and the name *Bubbie* comes out! I can pronounce the correct letters by stopping the leaking airflow. Totally wicked!

Once I was able to communicate by more than a board, Richard started in on swallowing. We still practiced daily, but our whole session was no longer consumed by relearning to talk.

We worked on talking exercises daily, but now we'd end the session with a few swallowing ones. It was sort of like training a baby to be a toddler but the "baby" was more fragile, and the process was more of a choking hazard. I had graduated to eating small pieces of food, smaller than you break up for your toddler, maybe the size of half a Cheerio. We started with ice cream, moved on to a small piece of banana, and then tried a sliver of a chip. Along with the fluids, mostly thickened, that he would bring to test me with, these were a treat.

Richard would leave me with "homework" to practice during the night. My tongue could barely reach my lips, so one of the exercises was to see how far I could stick it out: to the lip and then over my top and bottom lips. I couldn't reach my teeth at first, let alone my lips! But I'll be John Brown if I was going to give up! After a few days of really, really focusing, I mastered *that* challenge, and Richard already had the next one lined up. He said, "Can you do this?" and click-clacked his tongue. Well, I'll be. I couldn't. I practiced all night and in the morning when he walked in, I held up my hand and went *click clack, click clack.* He smiled; he could see my joy and feel my sheer determination to improve.

Right after my brain attack, my speech was, well, nonexistent. But when it did come back, it was little by little and very sloshy, slow, flat, and weak, without any natural rhythm or variation. It was an extreme effort to speak physically as well as mentally. It required a conscious effort to put thoughts into speech. Richard had to tell me what he wanted, and then I needed to have it not only explained but demonstrated. It was a very tedious process, and thank God *He* had already taught me how to choose my words wisely. It was strenuous, frustrating, and mentally exhausting to talk. *How could something that had been so effortless—so easy—before be so stinkin' hard now?* I often thought. The voice that I heard in my head sounded *nothing* like the voice that came out of my mouth. For a while when I spoke, I was continually surprised and embarrassed by the sound of my voice. I don't even like the sound of my own voice. It makes people quick to judge me even more, coupled with my limp and obviously disabled right arm. It's like having a speech impediment makes you suddenly stupid. Don't get me wrong; I realize I am very fortunate to have what I do, and nobody knows or appreciates it more than me.

I got the puzzled looks and "Whaaat?" from people a lot. People would often finish my sentences or act like they had understood me although it became apparent that they had not. You have no idea how frustrating that is. I found this very insulting and began telling people, "If you can't understand me, just tell me; don't smack me in the face with a nod and 'uh-huh.' It won't hurt my feelings, honest." I figured it was better to deal with the issue up front in an effort to make the other person a little more comfortable while getting my annoyance about it across and clearing the elephant out of the room. I knew I was hard to understand but found it very frustrating when people weren't giving me the respect to focus on the ongoing conversation. It breaks your self-confidence level more than you think. It's like you're judged and lose IQ points because, through no fault of your own, your speech pattern has been adjusted.

Chapter 12

A Hand of Grace

Starting that first Thursday, a pastor I had never seen before in my life came in, introduced himself, and began praying "over" me. It certainly wasn't *with* me; I didn't want to hear any of the nonsense he had to say about this so-called caring and merciful God. *Oh yeah? Well, where's your so-called God now? Huh? Don't get me wrong. I was raised to believe in this same God. I believe someone saved me, Jackson, and the doctors. Jackson is my God. Why would this almighty "God" set out to punish me? I'm a hardworking mother of two, a navy wife, not a murdering, drug-dealing gangbanger! Oh my goodness, will somebody please just make him shut up and leave!* There was no one there but him and me. I had no way to communicate with this stranger, no way of conveying to him, *Look, buddy, you are so preaching up the wrong tree.* So here I was forced to listen, with no way to shut my ears or run away. I was trapped. I was *his* prisoner. He had my ear, and he went on and on and on ...

Every Thursday for forty-five minutes, this pastor, this stranger, would take time out of his day, even on the snowiest of days, to travel from some church in small-town America to visit *me*.

The first two times I saw him, I dreaded it. I tried my best to tune him out—without success, I might add.

The third time he came to visit, I was having a bad day. I was sad, I missed my family, and I just wasn't in the mood. He said something about struggle and pain, and I lost it; I started bawling like a newborn baby. Now remember, when I cry, I howl like a wounded moose. And howl I did. And do you know what he did? He grabbed my lifeless right hand and said, "Is the pain too much? Are you ready to give it to the Lord Jesus Christ as your savior?" I managed to nod my head yes in the midst of my tears, and he prayed with me.

After he left, I thought about what had just happened and concluded that I already had faith. I knew that I hadn't made it through three strokes alone when the doctors and medical professionals who go to school for this junk had no good way to explain why I was alive. Actually, they had no reason at all, and only two believed I'd recover enough to be more than a locked-in vegetable. All the odds were stacked against me, so why did I believe that not only could I do it but I would? It was more than belief; I knew it, in every ounce of my being. I *am* going to get better; I *will* go home to my family again. I *will*.

That pastor visited me every Thursday, sometimes in time to meet with my family, until I was released. My favorite story to this day is the story of Joseph. When I was released, he came and visited my family and me at home.

Do you see it? Is any of it falling into order, lining up? Watch: it will.

The therapists, as a group, had decided that the time had come for me to leave the protective four walls of my room. It would be good for me to come down to the gyms as well as to Richard's office. It was time to see how well my body could tolerate standing.

Aubree was in Connecticut for work and had driven the four hours to come see me when in walked two therapists with this god-awful contraption known to most as a tilt table. Aubree could read the sheer terror in my eyes. She was the only one besides my mom and Jackson to even bother with picking up the board and trying to communicate with me.

They transferred me to this board, strapped me on it so

I wouldn't fall, and began to lift me, slowly standing me up straight. I was hot—so hot and so fearful. The terror started to take over and the "what-ifs" started to sink in. Mainly I worried that they would stand me up and I'd fall flat on my face, unable to stick my hands out to catch myself. Now, I was strapped in, and I wasn't going anywhere, but my brain's logic was overridden by panic. I looked over to Aubree with terror on my face and she said, "Are you okay shug?"

And that was it: I lost it. I started howling, and the tears started pouring. My therapists, who were subbing for Mary Katherine and Rachael, were engulfed in their own conversation. They looked over at my red terror-stricken face and said, "Peyton, you're okay. Are you in pain"? *No, but I'm hot and I'm scared of the unknown. I haven't stood in months. What if I don't remember how? What if I can't …?* They lowered me a little and let my heart rate calm, and then back up I went, no matter how scared I was. Being scared and nervous was to be expected. I was safe; they just didn't want my panic-stricken heart to freak out and cause itself to have a heart attack.

These terrorizing drills continued for a few days, and then it was time—time to head down to the parallel bars. *Let's see if I can do this for real. Let's do this! We get to the door, my feet are about to be exposed to the hallway, but wait: do I have to go out in public? Seen by all? Well, all here … humiliation … panic … I-I-I can't possibly!*

The train of people came to a stop. We had to deal with my panic attack for a moment before we could proceed down the hall a few feet away. *Okay, breathe. I can do this. I'm ready, ready to try again.* We proceeded down the hall and around the left corner to Mary Katherine's gym. *Whew, okay we're here.* I looked around and saw I was the youngest one there by at least fifty years. This didn't make me feel better; it made me stand out. I didn't want to stand out, to be noticed. I wanted to disappear. *This is just great; this should be fun. Nothing like humiliating yourself in front of people.*

Okay, there are like five people in this gym, including my two therapists and me. My brain's logic and reasoning needs some serious help retraining, but this is ridiculous. Yes, yes, it is. But I can't control when that panic-stricken terror comes on, so my only option is to go along with these "moments"—give in to them if you will.

The other therapists and their patient headed out and we got to work. Mary Katherine placed my wheelchair in the middle of the parallel bars as Jackson cheered me on from the side. Rachael stretched the fingers on my right hand open and placed them around the metal bars. Mary Katherine grabbed a chair and showed me the muscles to use, how she wanted me to use them, and how to get to the standing position.

I used the tone in my hands to my advantage to tightly clench the bars with my hands. Rachael was on one side of me, Jackson was on the other, and Mary Katherine was directly in front of me.

Mary Katherine directed me to stand, using my grip on the bars to help pull myself up, assuring me that they were all right there to catch me and the wheelchair would be directly behind me when I got tired. I did it! *I was standing up!* I was ecstatic, the therapists were ecstatic, and Jackson was ecstatic. *I was standing up! Wow.* I had never seen that coming, I truly hadn't.

Standing up was great, but what Mary Katherine intended to teach me was transferring—how to help with transfers to and from the wheelchair so maybe I could get rid of the wretched Hoyer that always caught my stomach tube or pulled on my catheter. I'd learned to sit up and remain in my wheelchair with "perfect posture," as Mary Katherine would say, but could I help them get me in and out of bed or my wheelchair? *Hmm. Well, no stopping now. Let's see.*

Mary Katherine had me sit on the edge of the mat, using my left hand to help. I practiced lifting my bottom up, clearing the mat. Then I would lift my bottom up and move over on the mat an inch. Then we would use a board, and I would transfer from wheelchair to board to mat and back, over and over. Then from chair to mat and mat to chair. Finally, if the chair was close enough, I could successfully transfer from chair to bed and bed to chair.

Then Mary Katherine would have me sit on the very edge of the mat, rocking back and forth, back and forth, to pick up momentum. In the midst of one of my forward thrusts, she had me push, push, push into a forward stance. My calves stopped me from falling backward as they sprang back against the mat. I did it; I was standing up from a seated position.

We tried standing at the parallel bars while Rachael manipulated my right hand and Mary Katherine made me reach left and then across my body to my right for different things.

Next we did the craziest thing of all. I took a step forward and then another. *Oh my word! Shut the front door! I am stepping! Awesomeness!* I was stepping, but the right foot was dragging, literally dragging, behind me.

Mary Katherine had an idea. She had a friend at Memorial Hospital who has recently been working with people on the treadmill with a new harness device. She planned to call her and ask her to come by and show us just how this bad boy worked.

Ellen swung by and they got me all suited up. They sat me down on the mat, placed a harness behind me, laid me down, folded a blanket on top of me to protect my stomach tube, and squeezed this contraption tightly shut. Then they hooked me to this machine and pulled me up and helped to steady and guide me as we walked with this rolling device over to the treadmill. They helped me get on and begin the treadmill, starting off super, super slow. I managed to walk five steps! Five! Yay! Success! Now that Mary Katherine had seen Ellen strap me up, she was ready to do it the next time.

Chapter 13

Going Home

Richard had been working with me on swallowing, little by little, retraining the pathways to my brain and that whole swallowing mechanism that we don't even think about and take for granted daily.

Well, the time had come to put all that practice to the test—the swallowing test, that is. There was a rumor floating around that I could go home sometime next month, but to do that, I needed to pass the swallowing test so I'd be able to give my body the nourishment it needed without the full-on use of my stomach tube. It would be there to supplement, if by chance I couldn't get all that I needed, but the goal was to wean me off the need for constant feedings. And by the grace of God, *this* test was going to be the deciding factor.

It all had to be recorded on a special camera or film or something, I didn't know exactly, but Richard needed to be able to capture me swallowing different things in a way that he'd be able to tell if they cleared fully and successfully. They took me to some room and sat me in a chair with this X-ray-like device focused at my mouth and throat to capture the chewing and then the swallowing. The technician, Jackson, and Dr. Pierce were behind a wall divider to my left, and I was in the chair, with the camera directly to my left and Richard in front of me, feeding me different bites of food.

No pressure. Months of work are literally at your fingertips. This will decide whether you get to start on pureed food and go home next month.

But hey, don't be nervous. It's just you, me, and this silly device, and people watching and holding their breath a little and hoping everything goes right. No pressure. Right.

I'm super-excited and nervous all at the same time. I know what this means, know how important it is. (Even now, writing this, my fingers are jumping over jumbled keys, and the butterflies in my arms and chest are incredibly anxious, trying to get out.) *It's an intense moment. Whew. Breathe. Just breathe.*

So we proceeded. Richard was giving me minuscule bites of this and that, and then we came to the chip. It was a full-on corner, bigger than I was used to, bigger than I liked, bigger than I was accustomed to. Chips were my archenemies. The jagged edges were too much for me to handle, and they got caught in my throat and made me choke. Richard knew this; he could see the hint of panic spreading across my face. He reassured me that it was okay, that I could do it, that this was what we'd been practicing for, and that if I couldn't, it would still be okay; it just meant we had a bit more work to do.

No, I know what it means; it means I can't go home. It means I fail. I will not fall victim to some chip. Bring it on! I can do this. I know I can.

He gave me the corner fragment of a cheese Dorito he had broken off. Moment of truth: Would I be defeated by some chip?

And it goes down successfully without a hitch! Yes! Wahoo! I got this; I knew I could do it! Bring it on, Richard. What next?

Apple juice—regular unthickened apple juice. I was thirsty and ready for that refreshing, smooth coldness that hits your lips, but not if it was unthickened. I don't fare well with unthickened anything. Water makes me choke. It's too thin for me to handle properly. Oh boy.

Richard warns me that to do the test, we can't use the thickened apple juice. Okay, momentary panic. It's all good. I can do this, Richard—let's do this!

The apple juice went down, quite surprisingly, without a hitch. Which brought us proudly to the grand finale. Drumroll, please … a banana. That's right, a banana. The size you would break off for your toddler to have, maybe two inches. *Wait, what? Two inches! What is with these sizes! Everything is more than I'm used to. This is it: the deciding factor that determines whether or not I get to taste my dinner. Survey says … yes, yes, I do! Oh my goodness, I did it! Shut the front door! I completed the swallowing test. I passed! I get to have dinner, like real food, no tube feeding, for dinner! Wahoo! And I get to go home next month! This is the best day ever!*

This is it. Food!

They brought me in my dinner menu, modified, of course, and Richard helped me pick dinner. Beef tips and mashed potatoes—real food, human food, food I could taste on my lips. They brought it in, and the nurse sat off to my side, because I was a swallow risk. I needed someone in the room at all times when I was eating, just to monitor, just in case.

I remove the top. What the … What on God's green earth is this? Where's the texture? The definition? I thought I had graduated. I thought I had just proved I could handle people food, human food. Not … not this. This is brown and white mush; literally, there's no texture. If I hadn't known what it was, I wouldn't have known what it was, feel me?

Oh, I graduated, all right. To people food, human people food, severely pureed human people food. We're talking put in the thing and hit go until it became a little thicker than water. But hey, whatever. I hadn't had a real meal in months. This "semi-real" would do just fine.

So I awkwardly picked up my spoon and dug in. First thing I noticed was that I'm so not left-handed. Second, this is pretty good. *I think I'm going to like this. Mmm. Food. On my lips, passing through to my belly, not just being poured through a tube and skipping the whole taste process. I can't wait to do it again!* I finished and excitedly ordered from the breakfast menu. *Mmm, blueberry muffin. Yes, I reckon I will. That sounds delicious! I can't wait for breakfast!*

Finally, it was time. I was helped into the chair, and the table was pulled up: breakfast!

Say what! I ordered a blueberry muffin. Now, I know my brains a little coo-coo-ca-chu right now, but that ain't no blueberry muffin. Sure it's blue, but it's, it's ... mush! Blue mush. I mean, have you ever seen a pureed blueberry muffin? How do they even do that? It's a muffin! It's supposed to crumble!

Ugh. Well, at least it's food, I think, and I get to taste and experience it, and this ever-so-annoying and in-the-way stomach tube is only being flushed with water.

To be completely honest, that's the best blueberry muffin I have ever had. It was delicious! Mmm. I loved this whole eating thing; it was great. I love food. It's so yummy!

This is it. The day I have been waiting for, the one I have been working so hard for. I get to go home! As in, sleep in the same bed as my husband, a room away from my children. I get to see them during the day, every day, not just forty-five minutes once a week. Shut the front door! Oh my goodness!

So why am I so nervous? What if something goes wrong? I won't have my nurses with me, the nurses' station five feet from my room, the morning doctor checkups.

I had a panic attack with my nurse Marie, crying hysterically. She assured me that the fear was normal, the house and family were prepared for me, and everything would be fine. I was allowed to be nervous and emotional; I hadn't been home in four months. It was time. Mind you, four months. That's nothing, right? You spend one day as a locked-in quad, away from your family and all that you love, unable to touch anything, feel the fresh air, go on about your life. Those four months were longer than you could ever imagine; I'd give you a time frame to compare, but I can't seem to find the right words. All I know for certain is that I wouldn't wish those "mere" four months upon my worst enemy.

The day I left, Jackson had a lot of paperwork to go over and sign. Mary Katherine put the security deposit on the special walker with holder for my right arm as well as my wheelchair. I knew I was going to miss her.

He finally got finished and we left. As we left, I recognized where I was. Hey, I knew this town. We finally got home. Jackson wheeled me in the upstairs. His mom had made signs from the kids with their handprints on them to welcome me home. They said, "Welcome home, Mommy. We will kiss your boo-boos." Too sweet! Too bad my two-year-old formerly mama's boy was still afraid of me. He ran past me, wouldn't come near me. And the baby—ha! The baby wailed and flailed and wanted away from me. Great. It was so great to be home, so great. What was the point? My kids, the kids I carried and worked so hard to come home to, the kids I had missed so much, didn't even care that I was there. In fact, they were frickin' afraid of me. Lovely.

Deep breath. *Breathe.*

I understood that Noah was unsure of me, and scared. I got that, I did. It's just that we were once so close, this hurt. But I would do anything for him, and if time was what he needed, time was what he'd get. He would realize that although Mommy may have come home broken, she was still Mommy.

My pit bull, Jasmyne, knew exactly who I was. It was as though she just knew the extent of my brokenness. She missed me; she wouldn't leave my side or let anyone within five feet of me.

Jess and Eli, my friends who lived down the road, walked down to say hi, and Jasmyne literally sat on my feet in the wheelchair and would growl if they so much as lifted their arms. That is what pit bulls are bred for—to protect. She did her job well.

A week after being home, I began home therapy. I received speech, Occupational Therapy, and Physical Therapy once a week each, on separate days, for forty-five minutes. It was a bit of a stretch after what I was used to, but at least it was something; that was all that mattered.

I only remember the name of my physical therapist—he made sure of that. His name was Dan Goodman. He was a really nice guy. That first day he came in, he brought over my special walker (it had a hand piece attached to hold my right hand) and had me do laps in the basement. Then he had me sit on the exercise ball. Pre-strokes I had done hard-core ab work out on one daily, but now I couldn't even balance on one. Dan would have to kneel behind me and hold my waist so I wouldn't fall off. He wanted me to bounce on it. That sounds easy, but it wasn't. Then he took me to the stairs and I started to panic. I couldn't even walk without a walker; how was I going to do stairs? "One step at a time," he said. "Take it slowly."

So there I was doing stairs my first day of at-home Physical therapy! One rail, on the right side; that's *opposite* of my good side going up. He said, "Wow, Peyton, you're amazing. Someday you're going to be on the *Oprah* show, and when you are, I want my name mentioned. That's Dan Goodman. G-o-o-d-m-a-n." Ha, ha, ha.

Dan was such a pleasure to work with, he had very high energy. I learned before the end of the first session that he was going to maximize our limited time and that I should never lose count. If you lost count, you had to start over. After that first day, I never lost count again—ever! A rule I still follow today.

I liked Dan so much that I expected the speech and Occupational therapists to be just as vibrant. They weren't, at no fault of their own. Neither of them had much to work with outside of an office, or the tools to do so. It wasn't their fault; I knew that. They simply did what they could. Besides, I would see them only four times a month, and then I would start my outpatient therapy at Memorial Hospital.

But speech therapy did help me to reconnect with my daughter. You see, Emma was also learning how to walk, eat, and speak. We would practice many of my facial exercises together as well as attempt to learn how to eat people food that wasn't pureed.

That's right: my exercises were mere games you would play with your baby. Moving your tongue from corner to corner of your mouth, pulling your tongue in and out and up and down, even scrunching up your nose; making all those vowel sounds and the faces that go with them, the click clack, click clack of your tongue exaggerating the facial expressions.

I mean, sure, it *sounds* simple enough, but this task was harder than it seems. The right side of my face is paralyzed leaving it rather expressionless unless a smile is literally forced. It also means that my tongue is uneven, more likely to sag to the right because the muscles on the right are weak. When we'd eat a muffin or banana together, both having to have small bites, mine would sometimes get lost in the black hole of my mouth, also known as my right cheek. I'd have to put a finger in there and fish it out.

At the end of the month, I tried my hand at feeding Emma the last of her jar food. Poor kid; she had more all over her face than in her mouth! I thought since I was getting off the baby food, now would be a good time to switch her too. Jackson lasted about two days pureeing food, gagging the entire time. It started the first morning I was home. He gave me my blueberry muffin, whole, not pureed or pieced, but whole. "I am not pureeing a muffin," he said. Two days later he ordered a pizza, cut a piece into strips, as if for a toddler, and sat close. I couldn't believe it. He was breaking the rules. I was going to get human food, people food, *adult* food. Yay. It was a complete success. I was sure to chew extra carefully because I didn't want to go back to dog chow, and I got to taste and feel the textures and feel like a big girl. This adventure was looking up!

Also by month's end my left-hand accessible electric wheelchair was delivered. It was blue with a removable seat and an, um, well, really touchy throttle. Let's just say George, Jackson's father, had a few holes in the wall to patch. No one's adult toes were safe. Hey, I'm not left-handed, remember? This was new to me—geez.

And more super-exciting news: Noah did come around! He saw Emma interacting with me, Jasmyne, his best friend, loving me, and this bright, shiny new toy that Mommy could give him rides on. Hey, don't judge. Noah came around in his own time, but he was still leery about the fact that Mommy couldn't pick him up or chase him and sounded different, much different. But he and Emma sure loved those wheelchair rides. And I was more than happy to have them near, Noah standing on the back and Emma in my lap. Ah, life is good.

Chapter 14

Outpatient Therapy

I made it home in time for my baby girl's first birthday! Yay! She was going to turn one, and we were going to have a little birthday party for her with close family and friends. Mary Katherine and Rachael from rehab promised to stop by too. I could not wait. I was simply ecstatic! I had barely been seen in this form—I was defiant about not going out in public—let alone allowing anyone to take pictures with me in them. I didn't want to be remembered like that. But today, I was going to allow one picture to be taken, so I might have one made with Mary Katherine and Rachael. They were more than mere therapists; they were my friends. I missed them and could not wait to see them.

I had started outpatient therapy that month at Memorial a half hour up the road. Jackson would load me up in my mechanical wheelchair, which my darling Mary Katherine had set up to go home with me till I learned to walk better, and we would head the half hour to the city for speech, Occupational Therapy, and Physical Therapy. They were forty-five minutes per session, and they knocked me out.

Occupational Therapy was first, with Callie. She was as cute as a button and sweet as honey. At first the poor girl could get nothing from my right hand, which was clenched in a tight fist.

Slowly, we were working on strengthening the muscles in my left hand with putty and letting the tendons in my right hand loosen.

Next stop, speech. Jackson would wheel me over and sit in the back corner. He was ever so devoted and wanted to be involved in everything. It was with Kelly from General, Richard's close friend. She had been called in a few times.

We would go into the gym and she'd have Jackson lay me down on an individual bed and we'd work on breathing—the correct form of breathing, that is. I had to reteach my brain to inhale while pushing my stomach out and exhale while bringing it in. I had been doing the opposite. By the end of the month, we were back in her office working on pronunciation and having Jackson listen. He caught every word; he prided himself on being the only one who could understand my every word. We would also try bubbles to test my breathing strength. Would you believe that even blowing bubbles was hard at first?

My last form of torture for the day was Physical Therapy with Ryan. Ryan was a sweet young man, a few years younger than me. It made me sad that he was only a few years younger than me, yet here I was in this chair.

We were really concentrating on getting my walking gait back. Dan had had me walking the first day he came over to the house, so I knew I could do this.

Ryan wanted to get me out of my wheelchair into walking. To start, he had me bend my knees and do what he called the "monster walk." It was hard; he started by having me monster-walk the parallel bars, with Jackson and the wheelchair very close behind.

Finally, we were finished. I was exhausted. I could go home, take a nap, and maybe feed Emma. Tough job, man: they were at me Monday, Wednesday, and Friday, for forty-five minutes each. I had a lot of work ahead of me, but I was determined to not be a burden, to pull my own, and for Emma and Noah to get to know me again.

Callie

Callie's main goal was pretty much to help me use my left hand. My right hand had been clenched in a tight fist when I started therapy in May. Callie had slowly stretched it open, and it was loosened just enough to where I was qualified for a device that would help stimulate the extension of my fingers. It was called the Saebo. I loved the Saebo, because it helped me extend my fingers and work with them in such a way that would otherwise have been impossible.

I also worked on my left side, not to be left out. My left leg was coming back to normal strength, my left arm and hand not so much. You see, I'm right-handed. *Was,* I *was* right-handed. Now I had to learn to be left-handed. It's harder than you may think. The rotator cuff was "sticking," and my elbow didn't want to move right, and oh, most important of all: how do you write left-handed? I didn't know, but I was soon to find out.

Rachael had tried once in rehab to have me write absolutely anything. She put the pen in my hand, but the whole feeling felt off. I thought I'd start with something "simple"—an *O* maybe. Looked simple enough, sounded simple enough, right? Ha! You should have seen this *O*! It looked more like a jagged square than anything. And my muscles were weak, so they were weak lines, with no indentation in the paper.

Well, Callie, my superstar, decided it was time to try again. And like a kindergartner, I was copying my alphabet and numbers. I still held my pen as if I were right-handed; my muscles still needed to develop, so my handwriting was weak and squiggly. I had very poor control over the pen.

Kelly and I continued our speaking exercises. Every so often, she would hook up this TENS unit, which delivered electric shock—I mean stimulation—to my face, and let it run for the session while we were practicing. (*TENS* stands for transcutaneous electrical nerve stimulation.) We hoped it would help stimulate the right side of my face, which didn't seem to be noticeably drooped but was still, paralyzed. It didn't move.

Leslie and Ellen

I was finished with my monster walking, so we went into another gym and met another Physical Therapist named Leslie. She seemed nice. She had me working on bending my right knee. Then she helped me to the mat on the floor and said she wanted me to sit back on my knees. Easy enough. Ha—was easy enough: *was*. Good God, when did sitting on your knees become *so* painful? I finally couldn't take it anymore, and the tears and howling began.

After a few weeks of that, it was off to the next gym and on to the next task. Leslie would have me go in the hallway and grab the bar and practice walking to the side, crisscrossing my feet. It was super-frustrating to know what she wanted and not be able to do it.

Ellen would have me sit on the mat with this big blue disk in front of me. I tried to rotate my ankle and keep the disk from touching the ground. They would rotate with me and what they wanted me to do daily.

My sweet little boy was going to turn three that month (July). How exciting!

Nancy had visited at the end of the previous month. She and Jackson got on well, which is good, because I was worried I wouldn't be able to keep her occupied. She and Jackson stayed up till three in the morning, laughing, listening to music, and playing the Playstation.

I know she's my best friend, so they say, but there's just something about her … I don't know, it's probably nothing, but I think she likes him more than she should, you know? Always reminding me how great he is, and how proud I should be, how lucky I am.

Note to women everywhere: trust your gut. It's called women's intuition for a reason.

By the end of the month I was showering with the children, washing them and me while sitting in a shower chair using the detachable shower cord. I'd also perfected putting in my contacts with one hand. Oh yeah, I was pretty proud. Jackson used to have to help me, so this was *huge* (in a singing voice).

Chapter 15

The Unexpected

Just four months after getting out of General's rehab center, I found out on my twenty-eighth birthday (in August) that my husband was having an affair with my so-called best friend. I found out while she was up visiting, surprising me for my birthday. What a surprise.

He had let me sleep in (until 9:00 a.m.) and then woke me by tickling my feet. I got up and got in my motorized wheelchair and went to the shower. On the way back, I almost ran over his phone. It was plugged in, charging, lying on the floor. Hmm. Lately he would never leave it near me, but always put it up a few shelves out of my reach. Brain injured or not, any warm-blooded woman would wonder! This made me curious and I didn't want to run it over, so I picked it up and turned it on.

Lo and behold, there were quite a few messages from Nancy on there. When we lived in Alabama he had always said he hated her, or so I'd thought. I read on: "I love you, Jackson." "I love you, Nancy." "Is she out there?" "No, she went to bed." Then the phone was grabbed from my hand. I welled up with tears and threw it at him. I couldn't breathe.

Imagine your best friend and your husband—the husband you have on a pedestal out of extreme gratitude because he stayed, because he cared. Even after all the strokes and rehab and being quadriplegic, he stayed … and then a smack in the face! What just happened? Did that really happen? I wheeled into my son and daughter's room where Nancy was staying and told her, "Get your things and get out of my house, you home-wrecking harlot!" We were living in his parents' newly renovated basement, so Jackson yelled up to his mom, "Ma, can you come get Emma, please? I messed up."

Nancy gathered her things and proceeded to leave the house. Unbeknownst to me, she went up and sat in front of the garage, waiting for Jackson to take her to a hotel.

He said he was sorry, that he had made a mistake. Then he grabbed Noah and said he was going to "take him for a drive." Later, I found out he had taken Nancy to the hotel across town.

The family had ordered me this beautiful edible bouquet that got delivered right after our little "mishap." I very uncaringly plucked the fruit off the skewers and put it in a dish for my son to enjoy. The day and the moment had already been ruined for me.

His mom came downstairs in disbelief at what she'd heard. She said, "I knew it was a bad idea to fly her up here. Jackson's in a weak spot." Once she had time to cool off, that mentality was quick to change. She was quick to become very excepting of the entire situation and her sons new pursuit of happiness. I felt hurt and betrayed on every level. But I don't blame her, honestly, I wasn't her child. I would like to think I would reprimand my son, maybe smack him upside the head, but at the end of the day he's my son. Wrong or not it is not my job to judge, but to be here for him, as it was hers.

I was hot with anger, boiling with bitterness and resentment over the betrayal. I just didn't understand. I felt betrayed, insignificant, stupid, confused, even more depressed, less of a person. I hated everyone. I hated the world. Most of all, I hated *me.*

The next few months were a blur. There was really no point in going to outpatient therapy anymore. We'd be in the middle of an exercise and I'd melt down crying, giving in to the pain and emotion. Nothing would register in my brain, my body would cease to produce what it was asked to do, and I'd end up leaving, having made the forty-five-minute drive to the hospital for nothing. Some days my driver would drop me off and in ten minutes I'd be back, ready, so ready, to go home. Sometimes I'd melt down in the car, on the ride. A few weeks of that—driving there only to have a public meltdown—and I needed a week off, for nothing more than to face reality.

When I say I had a meltdown, I need you to remember I had suffered a brain attack, three of them. I'd had three traumatic brain injuries classified as strokes not so many months earlier—eight, to be exact. The brain stem controls not only your ability to communicate and function properly, but your emotions too. And mine were still ever so fragile. They were in the very beginning of a rewiring process. I hadn't learned to control them or turn them off once they started. I had no control over them or when they'd decide to rear their ugly heads. I didn't just sob quietly in some corner. Oh no: when it came on, it came like a freight train without warning in the early morning fog. It was this loud, uncontrollable, wailing, moaning howl. Good glory to God, you would have thought someone was physically harming me. I mean, I was simply crushed on the inside, and that was just what it sounded like coming out.

It was more than simply "embarrassing." It was horrifying to be sitting on a mat, in a gym bustling with people, and just lose it without a single ounce of control. The Physical Therapist could have said, "Let's try that again" and bam, white-water rapids. When my emotions went haywire, so did my extremities. Picture this: my right arm tightened, T-rexing it-completely bent in and up, taking my now clenched fist to my chin. And my foot turned in to the left, turning under so I was standing on the right outer edge of my foot, which made it impossible to walk, even with my quad cane. So I was not only humiliated by the petrifying sounds coming out of my mouth, but trapped. I was quite literally unable to move. One, I couldn't focus on anything through the tears, and two, wouldn't you know it, my bloody body didn't seem to operate during a bloody "episode."

What gives! Seriously! The strokes, then Jackson *and that bloody harlot, and now this! Mortified in public! Why can't I just grieve in peace? Mourn my losses, which just keep accumulating, alone? I just want to be alone, without the scrutiny of the public eye. I don't like this new version of the world or the people in it! I just wish I could disappear. Woe is me is right: this is too stinkin' hard!*

Yep, you guessed it. Down, down, down I sank, deeper and deeper into the pit of despair. And on top of that, these ginormous dark clouds, bearing thunderous rain, just wouldn't let up. Trying to act fine when I was outright beyond miserable was impossible for me. I was terrible at hiding my emotions; they were traitors, on the list of those that couldn't be trusted. First there were the sad, bitter feelings, and then they were followed by the welling up of tears, the howls, and over-brimming flash floods. I was a hot mess.

I had meltdowns often, out of nowhere, in front of my now three-year-old, who would run upstairs screaming, all concerned, "Daddy, Mommy's crying again." I just couldn't make it stop. Jackson would come down, all kinds of annoyed. "Really, Peyton? Really? You want our son to see you like this, crying for no reason? You've got to pull it together. This is ridiculous."

By the end of the summer, Jackson had decided it would be best if he moved to the spare room upstairs with his parents while the two children and I remained downstairs in the basement.

Afraid of being alone, I thought it was a horrible idea. I didn't know how to be Peyton yet, let alone a mom.

Chapter 16

A Period of Adjustment

His mom returned to work that September. That meant I was left to take care of a one-year-old and a three-year-old while everybody got to continue on with their lives, going to work.

His dad, George, worked across town. Jackson got granted special leave from the navy for my severe condition, which also came with special privileges. He could go to work for the military in a specialized department that worked with George.

Jackson had been going back slowly, half days and such, but now that he was going back to full-time, I was left to completely fend for myself and the kids.

I could walk with a quad cane—well, kind of—and I had a motorized wheelchair. The downstairs living room and little kitchen were gated off right before the bathroom, which meant if I had to go, I had to move it. Easy enough; then I'd wheel right into the bathroom. I'd gotten good at more than helping make transfers easier, but now I could walk the few steps needed to complete them myself. I had learned to be fully potty trained again at twenty-seven, so I could do this, right? I could do this; this would make Jackson see that I was going to make a full recovery, that he didn't need to go off and be with a normal girl. I'd show him, I'd show him I could handle this.

The kitchen consisted of a microwave, behind a bar, with a little fridge and a little sink. My wheelchair could only fit in the small-mouth of the kitchen, but not through the tight opening. So I'd wheel in, as far as I could, then stumble my way, holding fast to the close counter for support to get behind the bar to fill sippy cups, grab premade bottles, and heat lunch—mac and cheese—in the microwave. Thankfully the counters weren't even an arm's width apart. I could hold on as I stumbled, right leg dragging behind me.

Bottles and sippies, you caught that? Yeah, my kids were three and one, which meant … diapers. This once-very-accustomed-to-diaper-changing mom had to relearn how to change diapers. One-handed. Awesome. That first day, the first time I had to change Emma, she had pooped. No big deal right? Except, how am I going to hold her bottom up, wipe with one hand, and rediaper her with a fresh diaper all while keeping her still? Ugh. Think, think, *think*. Aha—Noah. My sweet little boy would pick up her feet, lifting her butt so I could wipe. Then he would hold the diaper in place, stretching it across her belly, and I would tape it. The whole time, it was as if Emma knew this was hard, and she would be still.

Victory dance! We did it, we did it, we did it! I never thought changing a simple diaper would be so exciting!

Uh-oh, what about Noah? He was still in diapers. Emma couldn't assist me. What was I going to do? Who was going to help? Noah. Noah would lie down, and I'd undo his diaper. He'd then bridge, lifting his butt into the air, and I would wipe. Then he'd lower, I'd put the diaper on and attempt to hold it with my completely tightened T-rexed arm, and fail miserably. He would hold the diaper across his own belly, and I would fasten it. It wasn't tight, and it wasn't necessarily pretty, but who cared? It was on!

The end of the first day, Jackson came home and anxiously popped his head around the corner, without a doubt expecting a disaster. There I sat in my electric chair, beaming, while the kids watched cartoons, completely content. He said, "How'd it go?"

I replied ecstatically, "Great."

"Huh," he said, surprised. "Good job."

During this time three things became certain: I could do this recovery thing, my kids rocked, and Clorox wipes and hand sanitizer were my friends.

When his parents got home, the kids would want to go upstairs and remain there until bed. I was more of a babysitter, really. I couldn't be mom. My voice was a low mumbling hum. The kids understood me, but I had no authoritative power or sound. The slate had been wiped clean, remember? I'd pick up all the toys scattered about by leaning down from the wheelchair and piling them around me, and then go tuck them into the containers where they belonged.

The second day at home was easier. Emma had watched Noah as I changed his diaper, and when I went to change her, she bridged! She bridged! Having just learned to do that in rehab, I was in complete awe. She knew I couldn't help her do it, so she watched big brother and learned. She lifted that cute little tushy right up into the air! I was excited! How helpful! She stayed still, let me wipe her and put the fresh diaper under her, and then she'd lower herself onto the diaper and Noah would help me fasten it. Diaper changing became a family affair; it was great. Only with me did she do that. She knew … She knew.

As time went on, diapering became easier, and as we loosened the tight tendons in my arm, I began to hold the diaper down myself with my right hand.

Then I started cleaning the litter box, standing on my wheelchair to do laundry, and even vacuuming. Now, *that* was tricky—and rather tedious. I have only one hand, so I'd vacuum a bit, shut it off, clench the handle as hard as I could between my legs, and roll the wheelchair forward. Then I'd vacuum a little more and repeat the process till it was done. I had it down to a little over an hour.

Two weeks later, Jackson was kind enough to let me know

that as of the beginning of February, he would be reassigned. I wouldn't be able to stay there, at his parents' house, when he left. I could go with him, just not as his wife. He would help find a decent apartment for me and the kids. However, he wouldn't be living with us; he would be living across town with Nancy. They would be my support, and this way he could drop in whenever he wanted to and see the kids. *Okay, now I know I just suffered a brain attack and all, but when did that make me … Boy, you are outside your bloody mind if you think* any *woman would agree to that. Um, no. Thank you, really, but no.*

I moved in with my friend Annabeth and her family. They have an older house with big rooms and were kind enough to make room for me and the kids. They had one room downstairs and put two beds in it: a twin for Emma and a full for me. Jasmyne came and stayed with me too. They put a twin bed in their son's room at the top of the stairs just over me for Noah.

A week later was Thanksgiving. I let Jackson have the kids till bedtime, and Jasmyne and I spent the day together.

A week after Thanksgiving, I found an apartment five minutes away. We had been at my friends' for only two weeks. The poor dears had just moved us in, and now they were moving us across town.

I was so nervous. I had never lived alone. I didn't like this world, didn't like being around people. I was unable to use half my body. How in the world was I supposed to care for my toddlers, my dog, and myself? I had just learned to walk, damn it!

Breathe. You can do this. Breathe. Calm down. Calm down.

We moved across town into our very own three-bedroom apartment. Just the four of us: me, Emma, Noah, and Jasmyne. The landlord didn't allow pit bulls, but when we met with him, he seemed concerned about my being alone and allowed her. He knew where I was coming from, because he had had a stroke a few years back.

The friends who helped move me were so good to me. They helped me unpack and set up. They even set up my Christmas tree—too sweet. I'm blessed with caring, sweet friends.

The night terrors set in almost immediately. I'd wake in a sweat and panic every night. Sometimes, more often than not, I would wake accompanied by this sinking feeling in the pit of my stomach and my eyes brimming over with tears. Nothing seemed to keep those demons from stalking me in the night. They reminded me that Jackson had left me for a "normal" girl, one with fewer issues, one who could still move and was still pretty—and wasn't so stinkin' hopeless, worthless ... I could feel it coming, you know? I could feel the dark clouds looming above me and see that black hole forming around me, getting ready to suck me in.

This is it. I'm on my own. I need to learn to be responsible for more than just me: for rent and all the managing of the house that comes with it, and the two babies and how to be Peyton. I need to continue rehab, be a mom, be responsible for parenting. I have to strip off any remaining pride and accept any and all help I can get. I need to go down to the county office building and wait in line for food stamps and fuel assistance. There is no way I can do this on my own. I need help and lots of it. God, I don't know if I can do this, I don't know how to do this. I don't think I'm strong enough for this. Lord, I don't know what I'm doing! Good thing you do.

That first month my landlord must have visited me every day just to check how we were doing. The house was always a tornado when he stopped by, although he never said anything about it. In all my years, I had never encountered a landlord quite like him. I'm not a people person, well, not any more, at least. People are scary, judgmental creatures to me, and the less I deal with them, the better. I don't deal with people or the public, so this was very annoying to me—very.

I felt my world collapsing and caving in, but I couldn't allow that. I knew it wasn't all about me, and my rehab; it was about raising those babies first. But to raise them, I had to learn to raise myself. I had to learn a lot of things.

When being strong is the only choice you've got, you'd be surprised at just how strong you can manage to be.

I felt bitter, angry, hateful, and resentful that I was alone, that Jackson had left me to raise babies as a baby so he could go play house with a harlot. I was broken. I felt used and abandoned. I didn't know how to be Peyton, who she really was, let alone a mom. And me and God, we were so not speaking—or should I say, I was so not listening.

I needed help. I put the babies to bed one night and got on Facebook and decided to search for groups. I needed to talk to someone who knew my pain and anger and could relate to my frustration. I needed to vent to somebody who was as angry at the world as I was, who wouldn't look at me with pity in their eyes. I stumbled across this site "Strokes Suck"; God delivered me a sweet hand. I joined the little 200-person group, and Thomas Black, the founder and creator, thanked me for joining. We struck up a conversation.

I don't understand: he's so positive, so happy. Why in the world is he not bitter? Or at least angry and resentful? Mad at God? No, he's gentle, kind, and caring, ready to give and to help. He's all about God's healing. Do you know some secret I don't? Find the positive? From where I'm standing, buddy, I can't really see one. You see, I may be frantic and spinning out of control, but *his* plan, God's plan, had never wavered, never ceased. He was in complete control. Like playing a game of chess, he was aligning all his pieces, molding my character into what he needed it to be to serve his greater purpose.

I was bitter and angry at the world. Tom could tell. The one I was really angry with wasn't Jackson or Nancy but myself. God ran a close second, though. I was humiliated that I had become a "disabled" freak and lost a husband to a "normal" girl. It wasn't that it was Nancy, it was that she was "normal," an everyday run-of-the-mill girl, useful and not covered with the shame of being different—pathetically different, I felt at the time. It wasn't that Jackson had left me, it was that he had left me *alone.* Alone to fight my own battles, freakishly different in a world I wasn't comfortable in, a world I didn't know and didn't want to know. I was humiliated because I was this ugly piece of broken, discarded trash. I felt alone, ashamed, and utterly worthless, pathetic. And God, well, he had let it all happen. I had stood up and he had knocked me back down. He was to blame, right? He had spared me from the strokes only to have me suffer further humiliation at the expense of my husband leaving. Right? I needed someone to blame. Anyone would do, because it sure wasn't my fault. Hey, I was the victim here, remember? No good could possibly come from this. *God, I don't think you and I can be friends; it's just not working. We're so not speaking.* Ever felt like that?

I couldn't collectively see all the pawns God was currently and had been moving into play. Do you see them? My, oh my, how hindsight is 20/20.

Like Joseph, whose story is my favorite in the Bible, I had a lot to learn. I was a piece of putty that needed to be carefully molded, taught through tears of compassion and heartache. I needed to learn that I wasn't my circumstances, but that like Tom and other survivors, how to be shaped by them, learn from them, grow from them, and teach from them—to work with God and not against him. After all, he is friend, not foe, right?

Tom took me under his wing, and soon I was talking to people in this on-line group who were feeling just as bad as I was and making them feel better. I liked the feeling I got from helping others out, so I actively continued.

I watched all that Tom did and how he handled himself with faith, grace, integrity, strength, and bravery. I found my own self to be broken, pitiful, angry, ashamed, utterly humiliated, and, worst of all, unable to change the circumstances I'd "fallen" into, unable to play the hand I'd been dealt. Full of self-loathing, I didn't understand how he could remain so unshaken, so okay with God and filled with courage and hope, and furthermore, able to spread it like a wildfire. It was disgusting. I didn't have the proper knowledge yet. I was still very much a victim.

Little by little, Tom showed me there was no way out of the hole except by passing directly through the eye of the storm. Led by the grace of God, he helped me find the way out before it came crashing in on me. He taught me that it wasn't about changing your current circumstances but about *accepting* the hand you're dealt and learning to live with it.

God hears our painful cries; he just has a unique way of how he goes about answering them. A long-lost friend or family member you haven't spoken to in some time, a complete stranger, a pastor at church who just seems to hit home with every sermon—that person who just "happens" to come into your life at the right time. Wow, what a coincidence! I think not.

For the first time in months, I could breathe. The demons were gone, and I found myself able to sleep, peacefully, all night. *I can do this. If I can help other survivors, well, surely I can help myself.* (Do you see that? "Inadvertently" I learned that by lifting others, you lift yourself.) Tom believed in helping others, helping them find peace with who they are *now,* not who they once were. To do so, you needed to mourn for your pre-stroke life and capabilities. You needed to grieve, for grieve you must, because you had lost a big piece of your life. Your story had hit a fork in the road, and it was up to you to make the choice, to decide for yourself: was it going to be a roadblock, therefore ending your story, or was it going to be a stumbling block that you would then use as a stepping-stone to your advantage? The path was set before you, but the choice—the choice was yours.

Choice. You see, life is all about choices, and those choices lead us to more choices and harder choices, and so on and so forth. The choice is always ours. We can choose whether or not we are going to allow our circumstances to decide who we are and make us wither away in some corner or we are going to stand up, brush the dirt off, and play the hand we've been dealt to the best of our ability. Tom taught me that we are not mere victims, powerless against our circumstances; we were survivors! God is out to accomplish a set goal, and although you may not know his purpose and may look around at your life and feel frazzled, you can rest assured that he not only has a plan, but hasn't even broken a sweat. That God uses the broken, disadvantaged, weakened people of the world, the "cracked pots" if you will, so that people will know, beyond a shadow of a doubt, that it is him working. All the glory goes to God. If he is for us, who can be against us? Blah, blah, blah, right?

I was down with the talking to other people, showing them how God worked in wondrous, mysterious ways and sharing my woe-is-me story, but seriously? Easy now, don't get all preachity-preach-preach on me, 'kay, Pops. I believe; what more do you want? You want me to see? Feel? I've had enough seeing and feeling over the past year, thank you very much.

What exactly do you want for me to see? See the broken, disabled, hot, stinkin' mess whose husband couldn't even deal with her, or the crippled piece of trash who can't walk or talk or play with her kids. What, Tom? What? What do you want me to see? Huh?

I fought Tom tooth and nail for two years about the idea that God would want to use anything from the likes of me to enrich the lives of others. Slowly, I began to see changes for the better happening in my life. Doors that were once closed were beginning to open. It was tough at first, turning everything into a positive, but after a while, every negative turned into a positive in every light on its own, no matter the situation. For example, "Ugh, traffic" automatically went to "That red light probably just saved my life." The electricity going out went to "Ooh, I get to light my pretty candles!" It became part of me, second nature if you will.

What is happening to me? I feel … different. I see things differently. This is weird; it's like I'm looking through new eyes. I became curious, curious about how and why Tom was so deeply rooted in faith. I mean, he had stroked just before me. How was he okay with being—I shudder at the word—disabled? What made him so stinking kind and gentle and friendly, inviting and wanting to help others become just as peaceful? It's all centered on love, he would tell me. What in the world did that mean? What did that have to do with the price of tea in China? I became intrigued. After all, he *was* right about the whole positive thing becoming easier and easier. *I tried that and it worked. He just might have a point here.*

Just as curiosity was enticing me, tragedy struck. My dear friend's mom suddenly passed, and it was extremely difficult for her, because her mom had been her best friend. I felt this strong feeling to go to her, so I hopped in my car in April 2011 and drove to Alabama. I dropped the kids off at their dad's on the way. I stayed with Rory for a week, cleaning, doing laundry and dishes, and just being there to break that forsaken silence when she came home. Oh yeah—now might be the time to mention that she and her mom had shared a house.

Chapter 17

A Visit to Rory

As I said, on the way to Alabama, I dropped the two kids off at their dad's house. Just before we got there, we were on the highway moving slowly when a car pulled up alongside me and told me my back tire was going flat. Okay, I was trying this positive thing out and believing the best about people, but I had my kids in the back and was *way* out of my comfort zone. Plus I was still working on this whole talking-to-more-than-five-people thing. I don't do people, yet I felt no fear, no anxiety, nothing. Weird.

I like driving, because it's the one place I don't feel noticeably different—to the unknowing spectator, that is. You can't see or hear my challenges; just looking into my car, you are none the wiser. This situation was impossible, though; I had to go talk to someone (a stranger) *and* get my tire fixed. Man, I don't like talking to people I don't know. I lose IQ points within seconds because of my limp and my not-so-perfect speech. I try not to do it very often and avoid it whenever possible.

So this guy started to fall back, but he immediately came right back and said, "It's leaking pretty bad. Pull off at this rest area. I carry a pump in my trunk. I'll fill you up so you can make it to the next exit." He was a businessman, dressed nicely, but my kids were in the back. We pulled off, the guy filled my tire, and we got off at the next exit and had a garage plug the tire. Wow. Thank God that man stopped me, because my tire wouldn't have held out much longer. So answer me this: Was that just luck? A coincidence, maybe? I don't believe in sheer luck or coincidences.

A short time after I dropped the kids off, I had to stop early and lodge. Seems April is prime tornado season in the South, but being born and raised on the East Coast, I wasn't in on this little tidbit. Traffic slowed, and then the sky got dark and even darker as clouds rolled in and thick white golf-ball-size hail began to plummet from above. Now, I may not be from the South, but being on a jam-packed highway crowded by cars being peppered by hail wasn't exactly the most comforting of situations. There was an overpass right there to the right. If I could just see through the dense, thick fog, torrential rain, and treacherous hail, maybe I could, I don't know, at least keep my car from getting all banged to pieces, maybe find some cover. There is no way I lived through three strokes to die on some highway!

I got to the overpass and prayed, "Please let me get to Rory, please." Just as soon as it appeared, it left. Traffic started again, and we moved two feet and stopped again. For two hours. The highway in front of me was covered in tree debris. By that, I mean trees that had to be cut with chain saws to remove them! The very next two or three exits were destroyed, completely devastated by a trio of tornados. Did you get that? A trio! Three! I was beyond terrified. Incredibly shaken, I got off at the next exit I could and got a hotel room. It was the only building with power off the exit. The gas stations, fast-food restaurants, and local businesses were all covered with debris and out of power.

Tornados had been springing up everywhere in the South in astonishing numbers. A trio of tornadoes had hit the area I was in. I'm from the East, okay? We have blizzards and snowstorms—but tornadoes! Oh my, heavens to Betsy, to say I was shaken would be putting it rather mildly.

I got some sleep and got on the road at first light and my, oh my, was I ever so thankful to get moving out of that town. Do you realize how close I had to be? Hail! I was engulfed in hail! I was in the middle of that trio!

A few hours later, I arrived in Alabama. I had never hugged Rory so tightly. I was still shaking.

One day I sat in the recliner, flipping the channels on the TV, fixin' to fold some laundry when it stopped scanning on Joyce Meyer's TV program. Now, Joyce Meyer is a Christian speaker who preaches on choosing to live everyday life. I thought about changing the channel, but there was just something about this feisty older lady and the way she talks. *She's hysterical and she's got my curiosity. I think I'll watch just a little.*

I watched the entire half-hour program. Then, every day I was down there, I made sure to catch her program. After the first one, I went down to the city and bought my first of six Joyce Meyer books.

Now I was really curious, listening to her and watching her daily. She had me at "everything happens for a reason"; I may not have believed in much, but this much I wholeheartedly knew. And, as Tom had said, "God uses the meek, the poor, the disadvantaged." He likes to use these people so that when you see them, you look at the changes in their lives and say, "My God, there is no way that was anything but the hand of God himself." It's like when you see a clean alcoholic or recovered addict. *Hmm, I gotta know more.*

Chapter 18

The Secret

I began to know the secret. I got it. It's really no secret at all. It makes perfect sense! Kindness produces kindness; positivity produces positive vibes and feelings and then opportunities and choices. Doors really do begin to open as you spread the wealth of this "secret" knowledge and start saying yes more. Life is filled with choices and is derived from the choices *we* make. They lead our lives. We live by these choices we make. From the easy yeses and no's, from the simple choices of whether or not to be friendly to the clerk at the coffee counter to whether to have that baby or marry that man. We set forth a ripple of events, a law of attraction, that affects not only our lives but those around us, because we're all connected.

Suddenly, I got it. The fog lifted and I could see clearly. It all made sense. It was all unfolding before my eyes. What had looked like sheer chaos to me *was* bigger than me, affecting more than just me; it was all part of a plan, God's plan. It all worked out exactly the way he knew it would.

Looking back, taking inventory, it was incredible. I get it. I'm not "disabled," no, I'm merely disadvantaged. I'm not pitiful, powerless, or paralyzed by FEAR (False Emotions Appearing Real). I'm not invisible, unwanted, or unworthy. I'm not completely unseen and totally insignificant. Someone *does* care, *does* see me, and knows my pain, my hurting, and he loves me. And if I look back on the journey of my life, he's the only one to never leave me. All I had to do was turn around and answer the door. Huh, imagine that. I guess the world isn't so dark and lonely and full of despair after all.

Do *you* see it? It was as if God had his hand tucked gently in the small of my back and was simply guiding me down a corridor, through doors, affecting the lives of others as he went. How selfish I had been. It wasn't about me; it was much bigger than that.

Think of the doctors and nurses and CNAs, therapists, friends, family, friends of friends, strangers, innocent bystanders whose lives had all been touched, whose course had been altered in just the slightest way, setting them up for something greater. It is phenomenal—the fruit is endless. From that nurse I had met "by chance," to, right in the heart of it, Jackson. Or that friend who was a CNA and went on to become an RN at a nursing home because of knowing you, touching the life of thousands, because she wants to be a voice for the voiceless. Jackson, without whose military insurance I never would have received the critical care I so desperately needed to recover and the medical equipment needed to do so. And without the "drama" with him, I never would have learned courage or strength or that I needed God. I never would have gotten the courage I needed to acknowledge my imperfections—to admit them, own them, embrace them, and use them.

No, it may not look easy from a distance, but it's as if it became second nature to me to not make excuses but to find a way to make it happen. If I can't do something, it doesn't occur to me that I can't do it; I just can't do it *yet.* I automatically think of how it needs to be modified so I *can* do it. For example, folding laundry, doing the dishes, mopping the floors, driving, making coffee in a hotel room—now, that's a favorite. I can't carry an uncovered glass across the room. I have no balance, and the water will shake and spill. But, ah, if I use a bottle to bring water over to the coffeepot and then have a to-go cup with a lid to drink—perfect. I had no choice but to learn modification and to become willing to accept help when I needed it (more often than I want to admit). I had to learn to be teachable. I can do mostly everything you can do, except there are going to be a few tweaks to the blueprints. Sometimes I can do only part, but I'm far from pitiful and powerless. I'm getting there. I'm preparing for rain.

I truly believe that people come in and out of our lives for a reason, an exact purpose, for a season, with a reason. And contrary to our selfish minds, it's not always about us. We each play a role in one another's lives, teaching a lesson or being taught one ourselves. Then when we've completed that task, we each travel forward. Sometimes there's a distinctive parting of ways, and other times we just sort of fade out, our part played, our job finished. Most of the time it's no one's fault but the lesson has been learned: the job is finished, and it's time to move on. Own the change and gracefully choose to move forward.

Take a look again at Jackson's role. He came into my life "coincidentally" and "by chance." He was twenty-six, too young to have the pressures of a wife turned infant again as well as two babies. But at that time when I needed him, he was a raging pit bull, getting done what needed to be done in that particular season of our lives. I do not believe in mere "chance" meetings or coincidences. Everything happens for a reason, everything. There are no coincidences, only God-incidences.

Sure, I could go through life hating Jackson, dwelling on the fact that he had an affair and left me and me, me, me. Or I can realize that he was a kid, a twenty-six-year-old kid who played his part and played it well. Yeah, he had an affair. So what? He was lonely. He made a bad choice, he's human. We weren't married all that long. He didn't have the years of love and compassion and memories to hold on to that would keep him sane and emotionally balanced, safe from any oncoming emotional attacks. He had two years! Two! That was a lot to handle for anyone, and we all know how dangerous emotional affairs are and how hard they can hit. Besides, that affair didn't break me; it was used as a *tool* to help make me into the person I've become today. Without it, I wouldn't be this person, in more ways than one.

Why should all the weight fall on him? Because he's the husband and it's his responsibility, he took a vow, and, and, and—and what? He's solely responsible, right? Really? He didn't take that vow alone. Life happened. Things came up. Immeasurable things.

When you are no longer blinded by the hate and bitterness of the grieving process, you begin to see the bigger picture. You see that when you make that sacred covenant with God, in sickness and in health, one, you don't expect to cash it in until you're old and wrinkled and have lived a full life, and two, without God directly in your life, you just don't see it in the same way. You don't see it as anything more than a sheet of paper.

It wasn't about Jackson or the affair or Nancy. At the end of the day, it comes down to *me*. Peyton. That's right. Just as in the beginning, it was about me. Not that he had left but that he left me *alone* in a new world, in a new form, and I was scared, lonely, depressed, and humiliated by the new weaker, uglier version of me. I was unable to do my normal running but instead forced to stay, to lean on God, to listen and obey. Forced to trust, have faith, take the next step without knowing where or if it would land. I was forced not to just say I have faith, but to exercise it. I had to learn what it means to walk my talk. It wasn't that he had an affair but that unlike me in my newfound state, she was "normal." She could run and jump and talk and, and, and— Not that he was with Nancy, but that he had the audacity to be happy! How dare he move on while I was stuck different and invisible?

Did you catch that? The ugly path of comparison I was embarking down? I hated *me,* was mad at *me.* I was quick to compare my newly disabled being with everyone near and far because I was disgusted with me. Nobody had troubles but me; nobody was as ugly or felt as worthless or pathetic or unseen as I did. I was comparing myself unfairly, unconsciously sometimes, to someone else or to too many someone elses. I was striving to gain approval from a sometimes unknown audience, forgetting that my true audience is of one and only one. He loves me, approves of me, knows me, and wants me just the way I am. He wants the broken pot so that all of his glory and light can shine through and he can show the world that it indeed had to be by the hand of God himself.

I needed to fix me, adjust my attitude, my way of thinking, see myself for who I am, fall in love with me, fall into the basking of his light. I needed to learn to accept the glory he was offering and live in it. No, it didn't happen overnight—far from it. The path is narrow, and few will travel the bumpy road, but man, is it ever worth the uphill climb.

Yes, it's as simple as that. We are all human, and not one of us is without blemishes. None of us is able to judge another man for the same flaws we carry, and by no means are we qualified to play God in the lives of another. How's that saying go? Don't be quick to judge the speck in another's eye while you yourself have a piece of timber in yours? Before you judge another for any one blemish they possess, honey, you had better be perfect. Look in that mirror again, because the only one I know who's perfect died on a cross for you.

This is so exciting: we have the choice to be involved on a grander scale. We get the chance to be salt, to send love and light to others, to choose how were going to affect those other pedestrians on life's highway. We get to choose what mark we are going to leave on this world when we're gone, whose life we just might make a difference in. We get to show God's glory, be a beacon shining his light for the entire world to see, reminding every person we "happen" to come across of his perfectness in us, of what he can do. We live by the choices we make; choose wisely.

I walk with a beautiful marble-bedazzled cane (hey, if I'm going to have it, it might as well be fabulous and stand out and leave its own mark) and a slight skip in my step. My leg is no longer as heavy as concrete. My right arm and hand are still severely affected by tone and don't work like a typical right arm and hand, but they serve their purpose. I have a speech impediment. I sound as if I'm sick. After a year of extensive speech therapy and three years of "on-the-job training" my speech has greatly improved. While my speech is still not completely "normal," it has come a *long* way from where it was. I'm grateful for the thorn in my side I carry. It's the least I could do. Some days it pulls and twists and tears at my flesh, but it is a burden I'm willing to carry.

For that, I am ever so grateful.

I speak comprehensibly, for the most part, but my speech definitely gets worse as the day goes on and is noticeably worse early in the morning or late at night when I am tired. When it starts to regress, Emma is the only one who can understand me, because unlike Noah, she's never known Mommy any differently; all she's seen in the past four and a half years are improvements. She never knew me before my brain injuries (yes, strokes are brain injuries). And it helps that we both learned to talk at the same time. People hearing me for the first time soon realize that they have to pay a little more attention and focus only on the conversation to understand me. Some care to take note, others such as the ever-so-helpful call centers of our instant-gratification society get irritated and try to hurry me along. Thankfully, it stopped hurting my feelings around the four-year mark. People are quick to learn that no matter how impatient or rude you are, I simply cannot be rushed.

Bottom line: Normal is nothing but a setting on the washing machine. So what if this is my story, my background? I have the chance every day to improve myself, to be love and light to someone's life. I have the chance to be salt and make them thirsty—thirsty to want some for themselves or to make them see that they too can choose to play a role, no matter how big or small or seemingly insignificant that role may be, in the life of another. Because no matter how big or small, they are all significant, every last one. They are worthy and seen and matter, and they are anointed with their very own individual, highly important gift, whether it is the homeless man you acknowledge or the person you smile at as you walk through the door. Simple acts of kindness—"God impressions"—have happened. The seed has been planted. What seeds are you planting? What harvest are you choosing to reap? Me, I choose love.

I have come to realize I am humbled daily because I am different. However, it has taken me many years to realize this. I can now look in the mirror and see the beauty that it reflects—not physical beauty but beauty as a whole. I am beautiful because I am different, because of my drunken-sailor walk, my speech impediment, my slightly bent arm. Because I am humbled daily, reminded of my blessings literally with every step, every move I make. I am beautiful because I embrace my differences, not stopping at plain ole ordinary but shooting for extraordinary. I can see beauty as a whole because I worked for it and it came little by little. I earned it, worked hard for it, and therefore I respect it. For the first time in thirty-one years, I like me, I am proud of me, I know me, I accept me, and I love me. Who cares whether other people see you as simply "normal" or different? Good, let them. Be different. Be extraordinary. Strive to stand out. Smile and wave because they are too judgmental to get to know you, which is truly their loss because you know you're good people. Be good people. Be good salt. Spread that good salt. Leave a "God impression" on every life you come in contact with. Make 'em thirsty.

In the words of Gandhi, "Be the change you want to see in the world." Be your own sun, carry it in your pocket, and share it every chance you get. If you don't like your harvest, honey, change the seed you're planting.

Be blessed and live loved,
Peyton

But by the grace of God I am what I am, and his grace was not without effect. No, I worked harder than all of them—yet not I, but the grace of God was with me.

—Corinthians 15:10 (NIV)

"The Lord replied, "My precious, precious child. I love you, and I would never, never leave you during your times of trial and suffering. When you saw only one set of footprints, it was then that I carried you.

The Foot Prints prayer—Mary Stevenson"

Indeed he did.